Book of Mormon Stories and Teachings
Simplified

Alton L. Thygerson

Professor Emeritus
Brigham Young University

Printed in the United States of America

ISBN: 978-0-578-45958-5

Table of Contents

Appendices

INTRODUCTION

What is the Book of Mormon?

As a companion to the Holy Bible, members of The Church of Jesus Christ of Latter-day Saints (also referred to as Latter-day Saints) consider the Book of Mormon both as an ancient historical record and sacred scripture. The Church uses the Bible, the Book of Mormon, and other scriptures in the Church's Sunday and other weekly lessons, in missionary efforts, in its formal education programs, and for personal study.

The Book of Mormon is an abridgment of a 1,000 year record. It does not claim to be a record of *all* those inhabiting the Western Hemisphere.

Why is the Book of Mormon named after Mormon? Using his name is appropriate because he abridged the 1,000 year history of his ancestors onto golden plates and authored a small portion. Mormon eventually passed all the records on to his son Moroni who delivered them to Joseph Smith.

The Book of Mormon is divided into 15 parts, called, with one exception, *books*, nearly all of which bear the name of each book's author. Twenty-three-year-old Joseph Smith, founder of The Church of Jesus Christ of Latter-day Saints, produced the book within 74 working days of translation and had practically no formal education (Welch, 10–50). He published the first edition in 1830 while living in Upstate New York. Joseph Smith said: "Take away the Book of Mormon and the revelations, and where is our religion? We have none" (Smith, 4:461).

All or parts of the book have been translated into 111 languages (90 of the full book and 21 of selections from it). Since 1830, more than 180 million copies have been distributed, and currently, over three million copies a year are printed.

The book's purpose serves as another testament of the Savior, Jesus Christ. The Book of Mormon is available in print, audio recordings, sign language, braille, e-readers, and mobile phone app. A free book can be obtained by using an internet browser and searching for "free Book of Mormon."

Who will find *Book of Mormon Stories and Teachings Simplified* especially useful?

It's for readers who want:

- A quick review of a story and its teachings.
- For the first time, to become acquainted with the Book of Mormon.
- Simple modern English.
- Uncomplicated and straightforward retelling of stories and teachings.
- A unique format to help recall the stories.

What is the purpose of *Book of Mormon Stories and Teachings Simplified*?

It is not intended to replace reading the Book of Mormon. Perhaps, after reading or even scanning this book, people will be motivated to read the actual book. Many who value the Book of Mormon even fail to read it. Despite believing the book to be from God, many have difficulty recalling the facts in some of the book's stories, including the people involved.

Complexity of the Book of Mormon

Many people who begin reading the Book of Mormon soon discover that it is a complex book (Hardy, 1:195; Nyman, 1:142–143; Thorne, 179–193). Its story is long, involved, and sometimes difficult to follow. It is filled with numerous details. The book contains 188 unfamiliar and difficult-to-pronounce character names, many of them unique and original to the Book of Mormon. Keeping individuals with the same or similar name straight can be confusing and difficult. Most of the place names are also unfamiliar, and their locations are totally unknown to its readers. Many reading the Book of Mormon for the first time may have difficulty understanding it.

Its language resembles in many ways that of an older form of the English language, close to that of the King James Version of the Bible. Both books use, for example, the archaic pronouns *thee, thou, thy,* and *thine* and words such as *doth* and *hath*; both use the archaic verb suffixes *–est* and *–eth* as in *sayest* and *maketh*. The Book of Mormon's extensive and repetitious use of phrases such as *and it came to pass,* *for behold, but behold,* and the word *and* at the beginning of verses can irritate some readers.

Flashbacks (going back to an earlier event) add to the complexity of the Book of Mormon. Neither the Book of Mormon as a whole nor the books within the Book of Mormon are organized in a consistently chronological sequence. Despite being complicated and complex, the Book of Mormon is remarkably consistent in all its details of events, geography, and genealogy (Hardy, 6–7).

Uniqueness of *Book of Mormon Stories and Teachings Simplified*

When dealing with such a lengthy and difficult book to read, *Book of Mormon Stories and Teachings Simplified* breaks stories into smaller sections through a process known as *chunking.*

The "chunks" make reading and understanding faster and easier. Each chunk has (1) a short subheading, (2) a cross-reference to the Book of Mormon chapters and verses, and (3) borders surrounding the chunked text with arrows connecting the chunks. How each story ends appears as the last chunk, entitled "Outcome."

Chunking helps remembering easier. Two simple chunking examples illustrate: (1) a birthdate 12291967, which is not easily recalled, is recallable by chunking it to 12/29/1967 and (2) phone numbers in a long string of numbers, like 8013856493, are better recalled by chunking 801-385-6493. Chunking holds true for stories as well.

Other unique features of this book, which help readers, include

- Simplified versions of stories
- Stories and teachings written in simple modern English
- Stories and teachings which are paraphrased (reworded to simplify)
- Fewer words and shorter sentences that result in easier reading, shorter reading time, and swifter comprehension,
- Bulleted lists (easier to spot)
- Flowcharts, tables, diagrams
- Concisely explained teachings (e.g., atonement, faith, repentance, baptism)
- Chapter and verse cross-references that match those in the Book of Mormon, for further study of the story

***Book of Mormon Stories and Teachings Simplified* is NOT**

- A study guide with questions to think about and answer
- A commentary offering explanations
- A summary of the Book of Mormon
- An outline of the Book of Mormon
- A compilation of *all* the Book of Mormon stories, only key ones
- A collection of the author's opinions, interpretations, or embellishments
- A substitute for reading and studying the actual Book of Mormon

It **IS** an abbreviated, condensed, shorter, paraphrased, and simply written version of key Book of Mormon stories and teachings.

OVERVIEW OF THE BOOK OF MORMON

Use this quick Book of Mormon overview to understand its story:

The Book of Mormon opens by telling about Nephi, a son of Lehi, who was a Jewish prophet (unknown in the Bible). Lehi foretold the coming of the Messiah (the Savior and King of the Jews) and implored the people of Jerusalem to keep God's commandments (i.e., the commandments given to Old Testament prophets in the Bible). However, the people refused to change, and attempted to kill Lehi. Warned in a vision that Jerusalem would soon be destroyed, Lehi led his own and several other families safely away from the city (about 600 BC) to prepare for a journey to a special or promised land. Lehi's sons returned to Jerusalem to obtain brass plates containing a religious record. Then the group traveled across the Arabian peninsula to the ocean, where Nephi was commanded to build a ship.

Lehi's family crossed the ocean. After arriving in the promised land, Nephi began recording on golden metal plates or sheets the prophecies and teachings of his father, which is the first book in The Book of Mormon.

Within 20 years after arriving in the Western Hemisphere, a division between Lehi's sons occurred: some followed the righteous Nephi, and thus were called *Nephites;* those who followed the two sons Laman and Lemuel, who had rejected the beliefs of their father, were known as *Lamanites.* The book tells of many battles fought between these two groups, and relates how for 1,000 years both the Nephite and Lamanite nations fluctuated between wickedness and righteousness.

The Book of Mormon tells of other individuals who predicted the coming of Christ, as well as the many trials and experiences of prophets and church members.

The central event in the Book of Mormon is the appearance of the resurrected Christ to righteous inhabitants of the Book of Mormon civilizations in the Western Hemisphere after His death and ascension into heaven at Jerusalem. The book describes Jesus descending from heaven, standing among the people, and inviting them to feel the scars in His side, hands, and feet.

As He had done in Israel, Jesus appointed 12 disciples, gave them power and authority to baptize and manage His church, established the ordinance of the sacrament (the partaking of bread and wine in remembrance of His sacrifice), and taught His gospel.

The Book of Mormon then describes the conversion of all the Nephites and Lamanites where Jesus had visited. His visit resulted in righteousness and peace for 200 years. Then slowly, pride and envy became widespread.

Toward the end of The Book of Mormon and out of chronological sequence is the "Book of Ether." Its 15 chapters report another group that scattered at the time of the Tower of Babel, centuries before Lehi left Jerusalem. This righteous group built barges and also sailed for the promised land in the Western Hemisphere. This group (known as *Jaredites*) split into groups, fighting with one another, resulting in their total destruction.

When the total destruction of the wicked Nephite nation became apparent, Mormon turned over the plates to his son Moroni, who completed the record. Before burying the plates, Moroni predicted that they would eventually be taken from the ground and translated, to serve, along with the Bible, as another witness of Christ.

"Much of the Book of Mormon deals with military conflict" (Hamblin, 1:162–163). Nearly a fourth of the book is about war. Guerrilla warfare could describe many of the battles [e.g., ambushes, raids, and surprise attacks (Alma 52:20–40)]. The Book of Mormon teaches that war results from iniquity and condemns wars of aggression. Until the collapse of their society, all of the Nephite military actions were strictly defensive. The Book of Mormon acknowledges that it is appropriate and sometimes required to take up arms in defense of one's family, religion, and freedom (Alma 43:45–47; 46:12). Those reading the Book of Mormon may think it is an account of continuous wars and overlook the generations of peace and righteousness. Moreover, there were not as many wars in the book in any one time period as in the last 100 years of United States history (Ogden and Skinner, 51–63).

The Book of Mormon's Challenge

The Book of Mormon invites all to come unto Christ, to keep God's commandments, and to learn truth through prayer. Moroni wrote words to this effect: "When you read this book, ask God the Father in Christ's name if it is true. If you ask this with a sincere heart, with faith in Christ, and if you are willing to obey the truth, God will tell you it is true by the power of the Holy Ghost" (a paraphrase of Moroni 10:4).

Many members of The Church of Jesus Christ of Latter-day Saints, including those born into Latter-day Saint families, trace their conversion to Jesus Christ and their commitment toward the Church to prayerful study of the Book of Mormon, and through it they learn to recognize the Holy Spirit.

Christ is the central figure throughout The Book of Mormon. Christ is called by 101 different names, an average of once every 1.78 verses compared to the New Testament's 2.1 verses (Black, 34). That is why members of The Church of Jesus Christ of Latter-day Saints "talk of Christ, . . . rejoice in Christ, . . . preach of Christ, . . . [and] prophesy of Christ" (2 Nephi 25:26).

1. Lehi Leaves Jerusalem and Takes His Family into the Wilderness (1 Nephi 1–2)

MAIN CHARACTERS

Lehi—A Hebrew prophet who led his family and followers out of Jerusalem to the Americas in the Western Hemisphere after the Lord told him to leave. Sariah was his wife's name. He was the father of Laman, Lemuel, Sam, Nephi, Jacob, and Joseph, and at least two daughters (2 Nephi 5:6).

Nephi—Lehi and Sariah's fourth son. He was large in size, strong in spirit, faithful, and righteous. He received a great deal of abuse from his older brothers, who thought they had the right to rule. He built the ship that took his father's family to the New World. Nephi was the prophet, record keeper, and founder of the Nephites.

EVENT 1: Lehi's Visions (1 Nephi 1:8–20)

Lehi had a vision, which included a book he was told to read. As he read, he felt the Lord's spirit. Because of the people's wickedness, the book said Jerusalem would be destroyed, many would be killed, and many taken captive into Babylon (1:8, 11–13). Lehi went among the people and told them what he had learned. He also told about the coming of a Messiah, who would save the world. When the Jews heard these things, they became angry with Lehi and wanted to take his life, just as they had been angry with previous prophets, whom they had stoned and killed (1:18–20).

EVENT 2: Lehi and His Family Leave Jerusalem
(1 Nephi 2:1–8)

The Lord told Lehi to take his family and move to the wilderness (2:2).

Lehi and his family left their house, gold, silver, and other valuable possessions. They took only the provisions and tents necessary to survive into the wilderness (2:4).

After traveling three days, they camped near the mouth of a river that emptied into the Red Sea. Lehi built a stone altar, made an offering unto the Lord, and thanked Him (2:6–8).

EVENT 3: Laman and Lemuel Complain (1 Nephi 2:11–14)

Laman and Lemuel, Lehi's two oldest sons, said their father had taken them away from their wealth only to die in the wilderness. They said their father was foolish. They did not believe Jerusalem could be destroyed. They were like the Jews at Jerusalem, who also wanted to kill their father.

Lehi spoke to his sons with the power of the Spirit until they began to shake. They stopped complaining and did what he told them to do.

EVENT 4: How Nephi Responded to His Father's Message
(1 Nephi 2:16, 19)

Nephi wanted to know more about God, so he prayed to the Lord. The Lord helped him believe what Lehi had said. Nephi did not complain or rebel against his father like his brothers did (2:16). The Lord told Nephi that he was blessed because of his faith and humility (2:19).

OUTCOME: The Lord's Promises (1 Nephi 2:20–24)

The Lord promised Nephi that if he kept the Lord's commandments, he would prosper and be led to a promised land, the best land on earth. If he obeyed the Lord, he would be a ruler and teacher over his brothers (2:20, 22).

The Lord said that if Nephi's brothers rebelled against Nephi, they would be cut off from the Lord, be cursed, and have no power over Nephi's descendants unless they, too, rebelled against the Lord. If Nephi's descendants rebelled against the Lord, they would not have His protection, and his brothers' descendants would be a danger to them (2:21, 23–24).

2. Lehi's Sons Obtain the Brass Plates (1 Nephi 3–4)

> **MAIN CHARACTERS**
>
> *Lehi*—See Story 1.
>
> *Sariah*—Lehi's wife and mother of at least six sons and at least two daughters. She came from Jerusalem with her family.
>
> *Nephi*—See Story 1.
>
> *Laman*—Lehi and Sariah's oldest son, who rebelled against his parents, his brother Nephi, and the Lord. The Lamanite nation was named after him.
>
> *Lemuel*—Lehi and Sariah's second oldest son. He joined Laman's rebellious behaviors.
>
> *Sam*—Lehi and Sariah's third son.
>
> *Jacob*—Lehi and Sariah's fifth son and first son born in the wilderness. Before Nephi died, he entrusted the religious records to him.
>
> *Joseph*—Lehi and Sariah's sixth son and second son born in the wilderness.
>
> *Laban*—He possessed the record of the Jews written on brass plates that Lehi's sons had been sent to obtain. An army commander, he was killed by Nephi.
>
> *Zoram*—Laban's servant who was persuaded to join the group leaving Jerusalem. He married Ishmael's oldest daughter.

> **EVENT 1: Lehi Sends His Sons Back to Jerusalem**
> (1 Nephi 3:2–7)
>
> Lehi told Nephi that the Lord in a dream commanded him to send his sons back to Jerusalem. He said that Laban had the Jewish history and Lehi's genealogy written on brass plates. The Lord told Lehi to send his sons to Laban's house, obtain the records, and bring them to Lehi's camp in the wilderness.

Lehi told Nephi that his brothers were complaining that such a mission would be too difficult. Lehi said that it was not his idea, but the Lord's commandment (3:5).

Nephi told his father that he would go and do what the Lord had commanded, because he knew the Lord never gives a command without providing some way to do it (3:7).

EVENT 2: Lehi's Family Needed the Brass Plates (1 Nephi 3:3, 19–20; 4:15–16; see also 1 Nephi 5:21–22; Mosiah 1:3–7)

The reasons given for getting the plates:

- They would contain Jewish history and Lehi's genealogy (3:3).

- Lehi's descendants would know their ancestors' language and know what the Lord had told His prophets to say ever since the world began (3:19–20).

- Lehi knew they could not keep the commandments if they did not know what the commandments were, which were written on the brass plates (4:15–16; 5:21–22; Mosiah 1:3–7).

EVENT 3: Nephi and His Brothers Obtain the Plates (1 Nephi 3:9–4:18)

Nephi and his brothers returned to Jerusalem (3:9). They drew lots to choose who should go to Laban's house. Laman was chosen and attempted to talk Laban out of the plates (3:11–12).

Laban became angry and threw him out of his house, because he did not want to give him the brass plates. He called Laman a robber and threatened to kill him (3:13). Laman escaped and told his brothers what Laban had done. They were all very discouraged, and Nephi's brothers wanted to go back to their father's camp in the wilderness (3:14).

Nephi convinced his brothers of another plan to get the plates. The four brothers went down to their father's former home in Jerusalem and gathered the gold, silver, and other valuable possessions they had left behind (3:22). After that, they all went back to Laban's house and told him they wanted to trade their valuable things for the brass plates. When Laban saw how much they had, he wanted it. He drove them out of his house and sent his servants to kill them so he could keep their gold, silver, and valuable possessions. To escape from Laban's servants, the brothers had to leave everything behind, which Laban kept. The brothers escaped into the wilderness and hid in a cave (3:22–27).

Laman and Lemuel spoke many unkind words to their younger brothers. They hit their younger brothers with a stick. While Nephi was being hit, an angel came and asked why were they hitting their younger brother? The Lord has chosen him to rule over you because of your wickedness? Go back to Jerusalem, and the Lord will deliver Laban into your hands (3:28–29).

After the angel left, Laman and Lemuel complained again by asking how can the Lord deliver Laban to us? He is strong and powerful, and has at least 50 soldiers. He could kill 50 men by himself; then why not us? (3:29–31).

Nephi convinced his brothers to go back to Jerusalem. During the night, Nephi told his brothers to hide outside the city walls while he sneaked into the city and made his way quietly toward Laban's house. The Spirit led Nephi, who didn't know ahead of time what he should do. As he came near Laban's house, he found Laban lying on the ground drunk from drinking too much wine (4:4–8).

The Spirit told Nephi to kill Laban, but he did not want to. The Spirit told Nephi again that the Lord had provided this method to get the brass plates. Nephi knew Laban had tried to kill him and had taken Lehi's family wealth (4:10–11).

The Lord, who sometimes kills evil people for a good reason, explained that it was better for this one man to die than for an entire future nation to stop believing in God (4:13).

Nephi remembered what the Lord had told him in the wilderness that if his descendants kept the Lord's commandments, they would prosper in the promised land (4:14). Nephi knew they

would not be able to keep the commandments unless they h
brass plates containing the commandments (4:15–16).

He knew the Lord had given him this chance to kill Laban, so ..
could get the brass plates. Nephi obeyed the voice of the Spirit,
took Laban by the hair of his head, and cut off his head with
Laban's own sword (4:17–18).

EVENT 4: Zoram Joins Nephi and His Brothers
(1 Nephi 4:19–38)

Nephi put on Laban's clothes and armor (4:19). As he went to
Laban's treasury he saw Laban's servant, who had the keys to
the treasury. Because it was dark, the servant thought Nephi was
Laban because Nephi imitated Laban's voice, was wearing his
clothes, and carrying his sword. Nephi told Laban's servant to
follow him and to bring the brass plates.

When Laman, Lemuel, and Sam saw Nephi, they were very
scared and started to run away because they thought Laban had
killed Nephi and was now coming to kill them. They stopped
running after Nephi called to them in his own voice, which they
recognized. Now, Laban's servant became frightened. He was
about to run back to Jerusalem, but Nephi, who was large for his
age and had received strength from the Lord, held the servant
from escaping. Nephi told the servant, whose name was Zoram,
that if he listened to him, he would not be killed. Nephi promised
him that if he came with them into the wilderness, he would be a
free man and not a servant. He promised to go with them to their
father in the wilderness. They wanted Zoram to go with them
so the Jews would not know about them because if caught, they
would be killed (4:19–36).

OUTCOME: Lehi's Family Are Reunited and Now Have the Brass Plates (1 Nephi 4:38–5:1–21).

Nephi and his brothers took Zoram and the brass plates back to Lehi and Sariah in the wilderness (4:38), which made their parents very happy. Sariah had mourned for her sons and complained against her husband, telling him that he was a dreamer; they had lost their home, then lost their sons, and were now going to lose their own lives. When the sons returned, the family rejoiced, gave thanks, and offered sacrifices to the Lord.

Lehi read the brass plates containing the five books of Moses, which gave an account of the world's creation, Adam and Eve, Old Testament prophets, Israel (God's chosen people), Jewish history, prophecies, a genealogy of their family's ancestors, and God's commandments (5:10–16, 21).

3. Lehi's Sons Return to Jerusalem for Ishmael's Family (1 Nephi 7)

MAIN CHARACTERS

Lehi's sons—See Story 2.

Ishmael and his family—The family of at least five daughters and two sons lived in Jerusalem (1 Nephi 7:2, 6). Nephi and his brothers persuaded Ishmael's family to join their family in the wilderness.

EVENT 1: Lehi's Sons Return to Jerusalem and Go to Ishmael's House (1 Nephi 7:1–5)

The Lord told Lehi that each of his sons needed to have a wife so they could have children in the promised land. He commanded Lehi to tell his sons to return to Jerusalem and bring Ishmael and his family into the wilderness. When they arrived at Ishmael's house, Ishmael liked them, the Lord softened Ishmael's and his family's hearts, and they agreed to join Lehi's family in the wilderness.

EVENT 2: There Is a Rebellion in the Wilderness (1 Nephi 7:6–7)

As they traveled back to Lehi's camp in the wilderness, Laman, Lemuel, two of Ishmael's daughters, and two sons and their families changed their minds. They rebelled and wanted to return to Jerusalem.

EVENT 3: Nephi Told His Brothers What Would Happen
(1 Nephi 7:13–15)

Nephi said that they had a choice (7:15):

1. If they were faithful to the Lord, they would obtain the promised land. They would learn later about Jerusalem's destruction because of the people's wickedness (7:13; 2 Nephi 1:4), but

2. If they returned to Jerusalem, they would die there during its destruction (7:15).

EVENT 4: Nephi Is Tied Up and His Life Threatened
(1 Nephi 7:16–19)

Laman and Lemuel became very angry with Nephi and tied him up with cords leaving him to die in the wilderness and be eaten by wild animals. Nephi prayed for strength to break the cords. The cords loosened and came off his hands and feet. His brothers, still angry with him, tried to grab and tie him up again. But Ishmael's wife, one of her daughters, and a son begged for them to stop. This softened Laman and Lemuel's hearts, and they stopped threatening to kill Nephi.

EVENT 5: Laman and Lemuel Repent and Are Forgiven
(1 Nephi 7:20–21

The brothers, now very sorry for being so wicked, bowed down before Nephi and begged him to forgive them. Nephi forgave them and told them to pray to the Lord for forgiveness, which they did.

OUTCOME

They all returned to Lehi's camp. They thanked the Lord and offered sacrifices to Him (7:22).

4. Lehi's Vision of the Tree of Life (1 Nephi 8; 10–12)

> **MAIN CHARACTERS**
>
> *Lehi*—See Story 1.
>
> *Nephi*—See Story 1.

> **EVENT 1: Lehi's Vision of the Tree of Life** (1 Nephi 8)
>
> Lehi told his family about another vision (8:2). He reported seeing a tree with fruit that, if eaten, would make people happy (8:10). He also saw a "large field," a "straight and narrow path" leading to the tree, an "iron rod" extending parallel to the path to the tree, a "dirty river" between the tree and a "large building," and a "dark mist" stretching across the path to the tree (8:9–26). Lehi also saw four groups of people responding differently in the vision.
>
> *See the tables on pages 12 and 13 for detailed information.*

> **EVENT 2: Nephi's Vision** (1 Nephi 10–12)
>
> After Nephi heard his father speak about the things in the vision, he also wanted to see, hear, and know the things that his father had experienced (10:17). Because Nephi believed in Jesus Christ, he would see the things he asked about (11:6). Nephi received the interpretation of Lehi's vision.
>
> *See the tables on pages 12 and 13 for detailed information.*

OUTCOME

Symbol from Lehi's Vision (1 Nephi 8)	Interpretation Given to Nephi (1 Nephi 11–12)
Large and spacious field (8:9)	The world (8:20)
Tree of life (8:10)	God's love (11:21–22)
Tree's white fruit (8:10–11)	God's love is the gift of his Son (New Testament, John 3:16).
River of water (see 8:13)	Living waters are God's love (11:25). Filthy waters are hell (12:16).
Straight and narrow path (8:20)	Path leading to eternal life (2 Nephi 31:18)
Iron rod (8:19)	God's word, which leads to the tree of life (11:25)
Mist of darkness (8:23)	Devil's temptations, which blind people so they lose their way and cannot find the tree (12:17)
Great and spacious building (8:26)	Pride of the world (11:35–36; 12:18)

Four Kinds of People in the Vision of the Tree of Life Based on Their Actions in Seeking the Tree and the Tree's Fruit.

Kinds of People	Descriptions
1. Those who start on the path to the tree but become lost in the mist of darkness (8:21–23)	Obstacles that keep some people from their potential
2. Those who hold onto the iron rod until they reach the tree and eat the fruit but, becoming ashamed after being mocked, they fall away (8:24–28).	Those who begin strong but later weaken and do not endure to the end
3. Those who never start on the path but go directly to the great and spacious building (8:26–27, 31–33)	Those who don't even try
4. Those who hold onto the iron rod and eat the fruit; they ignore the mockers and remain faithful (8:30–33).	Those who begin and end strong

5. Nephi's Vision of the Coming of Christ and Other Future Events (1 Nephi 11–14)

> **MAIN CHARACTER**
>
> *Nephi*—See Story 1.

> **EVENT 1: Nephi Sees Lehi's Vision** (1 Nephi 11)
>
> Nephi wanted to know the things his father had seen and believed which the Lord could show him. While thinking about what his father had seen, the Spirit took him to a very high mountain, where he received the interpretations of Lehi's vision (11:1–12).
>
> An angel showed the things which Lehi had seen and interpreted their meaning (see the table in Story 4). He also saw Christ's birth (11:13–21), baptism (11:27), ministering the people (11:28), healing people with all kinds of sickness and casting out evil spirits (11:31), and Christ's death (11:33).

> **EVENT 2: Nephi Sees Jesus in the Promised Land** (1 Nephi 12)
>
> The angel told Nephi to look at his descendants and his brothers' descendants. Nephi saw the promised land and its many cities and people. He saw armies gathered to battle and many wars among them, which resulted in the death of many people. He saw great destruction caused by earthquakes, landslides, and fire.
>
> Nephi saw the heavens open and Jesus Christ come down and show himself to the people. He saw 12 disciples, similar to the 12 apostles in Jerusalem, selected and ordained.
>
> Because of Nephi's people's pride and wickedness, Nephi saw his brothers' descendants battle and kill all of Nephi's descendants (12:19–20). After many generations, his brothers' descendants fought among themselves. Those not believing in God became filthy and lazy, and did many wicked things.

EVENT 3: Nephi's Vision of the Promised Land in the Last Days (1 Nephi 13:1–14:27)

The angel showed Nephi:

- The formation of the "great and abominable church" (13:1–9).

  Special note: The phrase does not refer to a specific denomination or church. It refers to any and all organizations (political, economic, educational, religious, etc.) that lead people away from God and His laws.

- The discovery and colonization of the Americas (13:12–15).

  Special note: Christopher Columbus fits the description of the man who had the Spirit of God inspire him to cross the ocean.

- Lehi's descendants will be driven from their lands and many will be killed. Not all of Lehi's descendants will be killed because God promised him that his descendants would always live in the promised land (13:14, 30–31).

- An international war for independence (Revolutionary War) with American armies victorious (13:16–19).

- The Gentiles bring to the promised land the Jewish record and covenants (known today as the Holy Bible), which the Lord made with the house of Israel (13:20–29). The Bible was "of great worth" and "contained the fullness of the gospel of the Lord" (13:23–24). However, many "plain and precious" things were lost through: (1) deliberate removal of text or portions of texts, (2) faulty copying and translating, and (3) incorrect interpretations.

  Special note: These few examples represent some of the plain and precious truths lost through time (Millet 639–640):
  1. The nature of God the Father.
  2. God the Father and Jesus Christ are two separate and distinct beings.
  3. The infinite and eternal nature of Christ's atonement.
  4. All people lived before they came into mortality.
  5. God has a plan whereby His children may advance, progress, and experience happiness.

6. The kingdoms of glory available after death.

7. The necessity of priesthood authority and the importance of the saving ordinances.

- The Book of Mormon and the gospel come forth to restore precious gospel truths (13:34–37).

- The Book of Mormon testifies to the Bible's truthfulness, that Jesus is the Son of God and the Savior of the world, and that all people must believe in Him and obey Him, or they cannot be saved (13:38–40).

- Obedience to what the Son of God tells them to do, as found in both books. The time will come when He will show Himself to all nations (13:41–42).

- Blessings received in the last days if people accept the gospel (14:1–7) and a curse if they reject it (14:6–17).

- The Apostle John (see the New Testament's book of Revelation) and others would write about the end of the world (14:18–30).

OUTCOME: Two Options from Which to Choose

Nephi's vision provides an overview of much that has occurred and will yet happen in the history of the world. It also shows that we must choose between only two options: following Jesus Christ or working against Him, and thus following Satan. The blessings promised in 1 Nephi 14 are available to all who choose to follow Jesus Christ.

A formula for learning if things of God are true involves asking God in faith, believing you will receive, while diligently keeping His commandments (15:11).

A description of hell is given (15:29–36; also see Mosiah 3:24–27).

6. Lehi's Family Travel in the Wilderness
(1 Nephi 16)

> **MAIN CHARACTERS**
>
> *Lehi's and Ishmael's families*—See Stories 2 and 3.

> **EVENT 1: Lehi's Sons and Zoram Marry Ishmael's Daughters**
> (1 Nephi 16:7–8)
>
> Nephi and his brothers each married one of Ishmael's daughters. Zoram, Laban's former servant, married the oldest daughter. Nephi's father, Lehi, had therefore kept all of God's commandments given to him.

> **EVENT 2: The Strange Brass Ball** (1 Nephi 16:9–16)
>
> The Lord's voice commanded Lehi to continue traveling in the wilderness. The next morning, Lehi found at his tent door a strange brass ball. The ball had two pointers, one of which pointed the direction to travel. They followed the brass ball's directions, which led them to the more fertile areas where animals could be found and killed for food.
>
> *Special note:* The brass ball's name, Liahona, appears later in Alma 37:38. Elsewhere (Alma 37:38, 43–44), the brass ball is referred to as a "compass." It is not like today's compass which is used to identify magnetic north. Instead, it worked according to the faith and diligence which the people gave to it (16:28–21; Alma 37:38–40).

EVENT 3: The Broken Bow (1 Nephi 16:17–32)

While hunting, Nephi broke his steel bow, which angered his brothers, because their bows had lost their spring. No food could be obtained. Fatigued and suffering from lack of food, Laman, Lemuel, Ishmael's sons, and even Lehi complained against the Lord because of their suffering and afflictions. Nephi urged his brothers not to complain against the Lord.

Nephi made a wooden bow and an arrow from a straight stick then asked his father where to go to get food. Humbled by Nephi's words, Lehi asked the Lord, and the Lord's voice reprimanded Lehi and told him to look on the ball. When Lehi and others read the writing on the ball, they trembled with fear. The ball worked by faith and obedience. Following the ball's directions, Nephi went to the top of a mountain and killed wild animals for food.

When he returned to camp with food, everyone was very happy. They humbled themselves before the Lord and gave thanks to Him.

OUTCOME: Rebellion and Repentance (1 Nephi 16:33–39)

After traveling for many days, Ishmael died. Ishmael's daughters mourned because of their father's death and their sufferings in the wilderness. They complained against Lehi and Nephi for bringing them out of Jerusalem—their father was dead and they had suffered from fatigue, hunger, thirst, and were going to die of hunger in the wilderness. They wanted to return to Jerusalem.

Laman told Lemuel's and Ishmael's sons that they should kill Lehi and also Nephi, who thought he was a ruler and teacher over them, who were his older brothers. The Lord's voice came and severely scolded them. They repented of their anger and wickedness. The Lord blessed them with food again.

7. Lehi's Family Build a Ship (1 Nephi 17:7–18:4)

MAIN CHARACTERS

Nephi—See Story 1.

Nephi's brothers—See Story 2.

EVENT 1: Nephi Is Commanded to Build a Ship
(1 Nephi 17:4–16)

After traveling for eight years in the wilderness, Lehi's family reached an ocean. While praying, the Lord's voice told Nephi to build a ship according to the Lord's design to carry Nephi's people across the ocean to the promised land.

When Nephi asked about ore to "molten" (heated) for making metal tools needed to build the ship, the Lord told him where to find ore. Nephi made bellows from animal skins to blow air to make the fire hot enough to melt the ore into metal so tools could be made.

The Lord said that if they kept His commandments, they would be led toward the promised land. The Lord also said they would know that it was the Lord who led them and saved them from destruction by leading them out of Jerusalem.

EVENT 2: Nephi's Brothers Complain (1 Nephi 17:17–22)

When Nephi's brothers saw that Nephi was going to build a ship, they said he was foolish to think he could build a ship capable of crossing the ocean. The brothers did not help because they did not believe Nephi could build a ship or that the Lord had told him to do it.

The brothers continued to complain about wandering for many years in the wilderness. Their wives had suffered by bearing children and experiencing all kinds of suffering except death. They said it would have been better for them to have died in Jerusalem rather than suffer so much. If they had stayed in Jerusalem, they could have enjoyed their possessions. They said Lehi and Nephi had misjudged their righteous friends in Jerusalem who had obeyed God's commandments according to the Law of Moses.

EVENT 3: Nephi Tells the History of Israel (1 Nephi 17:23–46)

Nephi compared their journey in the wilderness to the Israelite exodus from Egypt. He pointed out that the Lord had led them out of bondage, protected them, fed them, given them water, chastened them, and healed them. Yet the Israelites had hardened their hearts against God and Moses. He said the Lord commanded Lehi to save his life and family from future destruction by leaving Jerusalem. He reminded his brothers that they had seen an angel and heard the Lord's voice.

EVENT 4: Nephi Warns His Brothers (1 Nephi 17:48–55)

Laman and Lemuel were angry with Nephi and wanted to throw him into the ocean. As they were about to grab him, Nephi warned them not to touch him, because he was filled with God's power, and whoever touched him would be destroyed. Nephi told them to stop complaining against their father and to help him build the ship. Afraid, the brothers dared not touch Nephi for many days.

After many days, the Lord told Nephi to touch his brothers with his hand. They would not die but would be shocked. After being shocked by the Lord, the brothers confessed that the Lord was with Nephi. The brothers fell down before Nephi and were about to worship him, but he would not let them. He told them to worship the Lord and honor their father and mother.

OUTCOME: Preparing the Ship (1 Nephi 18:1–8)

Nephi, with the help of his brothers, worked on the ship. It was not made like ships using a man's design, but was built the way the Lord showed Nephi how to design it. After the ship was built, Nephi's brothers were humbled by the results.

The Lord told Lehi that they should board the ship. After gathering and loading a large supply of food and provisions, everyone got on the ship, which was driven by the wind toward the promised land.

8. Lehi's Family Cross the Ocean (1 Nephi 18:9–25)

> **MAIN CHARACTERS**
>
> *Lehi's and Ishmael's families* — See Stories 2 and 3.

> **EVENT 1: Laman and Lemuel Lead a Rebellion that Hinders the Voyage** (1 Nephi 18:9–10)
>
> After sailing for many days, Nephi's brothers and Ishmael's sons and their wives began bad-mannered merrymaking by dancing and singing in inappropriate ways and saying rude things, forgetting that God was taking them safely across the ocean. Nephi was afraid their rudeness would provoke the Lord, and everyone would drown in the ocean. So he spoke to them about their behavior, which made them angry. They said that they did not want their younger brother to rule over them.

> **EVENT 2: Nephi Is Tied Up, and a Terrible Storm Occurs** (1 Nephi 18:11–13)
>
> Laman and Lemuel tied Nephi up with cords and treated him very badly. The brass ball's pointer stopped working, and a terrible storm began. Without the pointer working, Nephi's brothers did not know which way to steer the ship and were driven backward for three days. They thought they would drown, but they still did not untie Nephi.

EVENT 3: Pleadings Did Not Help (1 Nephi 18:17–19)

While Nephi was tied up, Lehi spoke many things to Nephi's brothers and Ishmael's sons, for which they threatened anyone who said anything about helping Nephi. Lehi and Sariah became very sick and almost died, being old and sad about their sons' wickedness. Even the tears and prayers of Nephi's wife and children did not soften his brothers' hearts to untie him.

OUTCOME: Nephi is Untied and Arrives in the Promised Land (1 Nephi 18:20–23)

The brothers softened their hearts only after the storm became more threatening and they felt God's power could destroy them. When they realized they were about to die, they repented and untied Nephi. The brass ball started working again, and after Nephi prayed to the Lord, the storm stopped. After many days of sailing, they arrived at the promised land.

9. Lehi Counsels His Family (2 Nephi 1:1–4:12)

MAIN CHARACTER

Lehi—See Story 1.

EVENT 1: Lehi's Advice and Prophecies (2 Nephi 1:5–13)

Lehi said that despite having experienced many difficulties, they had been given the promised land, a land better than all other lands. God promised Lehi that the land would belong to his descendants and to all those whom the Lord would lead there (1:5–6).

The agreement between the Lord and Lehi's people was that if they kept the commandments given them, they would prosper, be free, and be blessed; no one would hurt them or take away their land, and they would live there safely forever (1:7, 9–10).

If they rejected the Savior, God's judgments would be on them. He would bring other nations to the land, and He would give them power to take away the Nephites' lands, and to scatter and destroy them. There would be bloodshed for many years (1:10–12).

Lehi told his sons to repent to avoid eternal misery (1:13).

EVENT 2: Lehi Taught About the Atonement of Jesus Christ (2 Nephi 2:6–15)

- Salvation comes in and through the Holy Messiah (2:6).

- Jesus Christ will offer Himself as a sacrifice for sin, to pay the price of the law for all who have a broken heart and repentant spirit. Only He can do this (2:7).

- The Messiah will give up His life on earth and take it again by the power of the Spirit, so that the dead can live again. He will be the first to rise from the dead (2:8).

- He will ask for mercy for all people, and those who believe in Him will be saved (2:9).

- All people will appear before God to be judged, because the Messiah will be merciful toward them. A punishment, which is the opposite of happiness, is why the Atonement is needed (2:10).

- There must be opposition, or opposites, in all things (2:11–13, 15).

EVENT 3: More on What Lehi Taught About the Atonement (2 Nephi 2:19–26)

- After Adam and Eve ate the forbidden fruit, they were sent away from the Garden of Eden (2:19).

- God allowed people to live longer to give them time to repent. This life is a test to see if people will keep God's commandments. People were "lost" because of their first parents' sin (2:21).

- If Adam and Eve had not sinned, they would have remained forever in the Garden of Eden in the same condition in which they had been created and placed there (2:22).

- Adam and Eve would not have had children. They would have no joy because without a knowledge of good and evil, they would know no misery. They could have done no good, because they did not know sin (2:23).

- Adam and Eve chose to fall from their state of innocence in order to have children, and even in this fallen world, people are meant to have joy (2:25).

- The Messiah would come to save people from the Fall (2:26).

- Because people are saved from the Fall, they are free to act for themselves, because they know good from evil (2:26).

- We are all free to choose liberty and eternal life or captivity and death (2:27).

Summary About the Fall and the Atonement of Jesus Christ

If Adam and Eve ...	Then ...
Had not eaten the forbidden fruit and not fallen,	• All things would have remained in the Garden of Eden forever (2 Nephi 2:22). • They would have had no children (2 Nephi 2:23). • They would have known neither joy nor misery. • They would not have done any good or evil (2 Nephi 2:23).
Because they ate the forbidden fruit, they fell.	• They were driven out of the garden to till the earth (2 Nephi 2:19). • They started to have children—the first family on earth (2 Nephi 2:20). • They and their descendants would experience mortal life, including joy, misery, and the ability to do good and to sin (2 Nephi 2:23, 25). • All people are subject to physical and spiritual death (2 Nephi 9:6; Helaman 14:16).

OUTCOME: Lehi's Death

After he had spoken to his family and household about the feelings in his heart, which the Spirit led him to say, Lehi died and was buried (2 Nephi 4:12).

10. Nephi's Group Separates from the Lamanites
(2 Nephi 5)

MAIN CHARACTERS

Nephi—See Story 1.

Nephites—Descendants of Nephi and his followers, including all who accepted the gospel.

Lamanites—Descendants of Laman and Lemuel, including anyone who rebelled against Nephi and the Lord.

EVENT 1: Laman and Lemuel Rebel Against Nephi and the Lord (2 Nephi 5:1–4)

Nephi prayed to the Lord many times about his brothers because of their anger against him. They complained that Nephi wanted to rule over them. They believed that because they were the oldest, the right to rule over the people belonged to them. Their anger grew until they wanted to kill Nephi.

EVENT 2: The Nephites Prosper (2 Nephi 5:5–18)

The Lord, warning Nephi about his brothers' plans, told him to flee into the wilderness and take those who would go with him. He took his family, Zoram and his family, his older brother Sam and his family, his younger brothers Jacob and Joseph, his sisters, and all others who believed in God's warnings (5:5–6).

They took everything they could carry and traveled for many days before arriving at their new location. The people called themselves Nephites. They prospered and had many children (5:7, 9, 13).

Using Laban's sword as a model, Nephi made many swords for protection from the people now called Lamanites. Nephi knew

Laman had taught his followers to hate him, his children, and the people who called themselves Nephites (5:14).

The Nephites built buildings and a temple similar to Solomon's temple (5:15–16).

OUTCOME: Wars and Contentions Between the Nephites and Lamanites (2 Nephi 5:34)

Forty years had passed since these peoples had left Jerusalem, and already the Nephites had wars and contentions with the Lamanites.

11. Jacob Teaches Gospel Principles (2 Nephi 9:6–52)

MAIN CHARACTER

Jacob—See Story 2.

EVENT 1: Jacob Defines Temporal Death and Spiritual Death (2 Nephi 9:6–12)

Temporal or physical death occurs when the physical body dies and the spirit separates from the physical body. All people die temporally because of the Fall of Adam and Eve (9:6). Jacob referred to temporal death using the words and phrases "death" (9:6), "the death of the body" (9:10), and "the grave" (9:11).

Spiritual death occurs when we are not in the Lord's presence. This occurred as a result of the Fall of Adam and Eve (9:6). Separation from God happens when we sin (Alma 12:16; Helaman 14:18; New Testament's Romans 3:23). To refer to spiritual death, Jacob uses the words and phrases "shut out from the presence of our God" (9:9), "the death of the spirit (9:10), "spiritual death" (9:12), "hell" (9:12), and "death" (9:39).

EVENT 2: Jacob Tells About the Fall and the Atonement (2 Nephi 9:7–15)

- An infinite or eternal atonement was needed to overcome the Fall (9:7).

- Without an infinite atonement, there would be no resurrection of the bodies of people—death would last forever. The body would die, decay, and become part of the earth, never to rise again (9:7).

- Without an infinite atonement, the spirits of all men would become devils, forever miserable. They would not just be subject to the devil, but they would actually become devils (9:8–9).

- Because of the Atonement, all people will be resurrected, that is, saved from physical or temporal death. Without the resurrection, temporal and spiritual death would be permanent—shut out from God's presence and our spirits subject to Satan (9:10–13).

- After the resurrection, all mankind will be judged by God (2:10; 9:15).

- The Redeemer, who will die for mankind, is also the Creator (9:5).

- All of these things are according to an eternal plan of the great Creator (9:6, 13).

EVENT 3: How to Be Saved in God's Kingdom?
(2 Nephi 9:18–52)

Not all people will be saved in God's kingdom or permitted to dwell in God's presence forever (9:23).

Some of the things we must do to be "saved in God's kingdom":

- Believe in Jesus Christ and come unto Him (9:18, 23–24, 41).

- Endure the world's persecution (9:18).

- Listen to the Lord's voice (9:21).

- Repent, be baptized, and endure to the end (9:23–24).

- Do not think only of worldly things, but think of spiritual things (9:39).

- Do not spend money on worthless things, and do not work for things that will never be satisfying. Come to Jesus Christ and enjoy His gifts of eternity (9: 50–51).

- Remember God's words (9:52).

- Pray continually and give thanks (9:52).

OUTCOME: Who is the Gatekeeper at the Entrance to the Kingdom of Heaven? (2 Nephi 9:41–43)

The Lord's path is narrow and leads straight to Him. The end of the path has only one gate. The Lord guards the gate, with no help from a servant. No one can come in except at the gate, and the Lord cannot be deceived. He will open the gate to whoever knocks, but He dislikes those who are proud of their education and wealth. Unless they give up their pride and humble themselves before Him, He will not open the gate to them. The happiness prepared for the saints will be hidden from them.

12. Sherem Teaches False Doctrine (Jacob 7:1–23)

MAIN CHARACTERS

Jacob—See Story 2.

Sherem—He taught that there would be no Christ. He was a powerful speaker who convinced many that it was blasphemy to (1) change the Law of Moses and (2) worship a person on earth yet to come hundreds of years in the future, and (3) know the future.

EVENT 1: Description of Sherem (Jacob 7:1–5)

A man named Sherem came among the Nephites, preaching that there would be no Christ. He said many flattering things to convince people not to believe in Christ. He successfully led many people away from Christ. He wanted to speak to Jacob and destroy his faith in Christ. Sherem was educated and was a very flattering and powerful speaker. He tried to shake Jacob's faith in Christ. Jacob had seen angels, had heard the Lord's voice speak to him, and could not be shaken.

EVENT 2: Sherem Demands a Sign and Is Cursed
(Jacob 7:6–15)

Sherem told Jacob that he had heard that Jacob preached what he called the *gospel* or the *doctrine of Christ.* Sherem said that Jacob had led many people away from God's ways and had told them to disobey the Law of Moses. Jacob had also tried to get people to worship a person who he says would come many hundreds of years in the future. This is blasphemy, Sherem insisted, because no one can see the future.

Then God sent His Spirit to help Jacob. Jacob asked Sherem if he was saying that Christ would not come. Sherem answered that if there were a Christ, he would not deny Him, but he knew that there was no Christ, neither has been, nor ever will be. Jacob asked Sherem if he believed the scriptures. He replied yes. Jacob then said that he did not understand them, because they talk about Christ. All the prophets have written and prophesied about Christ. Jacob said that he had seen and heard Christ in a vision, and by the power of the Holy Ghost, he learned that if no atonement were made, then everyone would be lost.

Sherem asked for a sign by the power of this Holy Ghost, whom Jacob knew so much about. Jacob replied that he would not ask God to show a sign about something that Sherem already knew was true. Even if Sherem saw a sign, he would still deny Christ, because he was of the devil. If God struck Sherem, that would be His sign to him that He has power and that Christ would come.

As Jacob said this, the Lord's power came upon Sherem, and he collapsed to the ground. For many days, he had to be fed by the people.

OUTCOME: Sherem's Confession and Death (Jacob 7:16–23)

Sherem told the people to gather tomorrow, because he wanted to talk to them before he died. The next day when the people gathered, Sherem spoke plainly to them. He said the things he had taught were wrong. He now believed in Christ, the power of the Holy Ghost, and in angels. The devil had tricked him. He spoke about hell, eternal punishment, and eternity.

He was afraid that he had sinned so much that he could not be forgiven, because he lied to God, and said there was no Christ. He believed the scriptures, and they testified of Christ. Because he lied to God, he was afraid for his future. He confessed his evil works to God, and then he died.

13. Enos Prays All Day (Enos 1)

MAIN CHARACTER

Enos—Nephite prophet, son of Jacob, who was Nephi's brother.

EVENT 1: Credit Given by Enos to His Father For Teaching Him (Enos 1:1)

Enos acknowledged his father for teaching him about the Lord and his father's language.

EVENT 2: Enos Received Forgiveness of Sins (Enos 1:2–8)

Enos told of his struggle before God because of his sins. Having gone into the forest to hunt animals, he began thinking about the words he had often heard his father say about eternal life and how happy God's saints were. He wanted this happiness. He knelt down and prayed to God to be blessed. He prayed all day long until night came. He then heard a voice saying that his sins were forgiven and he would be blessed. Enos knew that God could not lie, and his guilt was swept away. He asked the Lord how this could happen. The Lord told Enos that it was because of his faith in Christ, whom Enos had never heard nor seen.

EVENT 3: Enos's Prayer (Enos 1:9–18)

After hearing those words, Enos began praying for his people, the Nephites. While he was praying, the Lord's voice came again into his mind, saying He would bless or curse the Nephites depending on how well they kept His commandments.

He also prayed long hours for the Lamanites, who had said they would kill the Nephites and destroy their records. Enos asked the

Lord if his people, the Nephites, fell into sin and were destroyed, and the Lamanites survived, would the Lord save the Nephite record so that it could go to the Lamanites at some future day for their salvation. The Lord replied that whatever you ask, in the name of Christ, believing that you will receive, will be granted.

EVENT 4: Description of Apostate Lamanites and Stiff-necked Nephites (Enos 1:19–24)

Enos went among the Nephites, preaching about things that would happen. The Nephites tried to teach the Lamanites about God, but their hatred was strong, and they would not listen. They had become a wild, ferocious, and bloodthirsty people. They worshiped false gods, were filthy, and they ate beasts of prey. They wore only animal skins around their waists and hips and shaved their heads. They were skilled with the bow and arrow and ax. They were always trying to kill the Nephites.

Many prophets came among the Nephites, but they had become too proud to listen. The only thing that helped them keep God's commandments was the fear of the Lord after hearing about war, death, and the length of eternity, so the fear of God's judgments and power kept them from being destroyed. Many wars occurred between the Nephites and Lamanites.

OUTCOME: The End of Enos's Life (Enos 1:25–27)

It had been 179 years since Lehi, Enos's grandfather, had left Jerusalem. Enos said that he would die soon. All his life, God's power compelled him to preach to the Nephites. Knowing about Christ had given him more joy than any other thing. He looked forward to the day when he would stand before Christ, see His face, and hear Him say to come to Him, for there is a place prepared for you to live in my Father's kingdom.

14. Benjamin Speaks to the People (Mosiah 1:1–6:3)

MAIN CHARACTERS

Benjamin—A Nephite prophet-king, a son of Mosiah. He reigned over his people in righteousness. He is known for delivering a major address to all his people shortly before he died.

Mosiah—The son of Benjamin, he was appointed to be the king by his father.

EVENT 1: Benjamin Taught His Sons (Mosiah 1:2–7)

Benjamin's three sons learned their ancestor's language and understood what the Lord had told the prophets. He told them if it were not for the brass plates containing the commandments, they would not know about the mysteries of God. The brass plates helped Lehi remember the important things to teach his children. Otherwise, they would have been like the Lamanites, who knew nothing about the Lord. Benjamin counseled the people to study the commandments and keep them.

Special note: Simple truths are "mysteries" to those who do not have an understanding of the gospel of Jesus Christ (see Story 46, Event 2). The term does not refer to mysterious, secretive, and unknown things. The mysteries (the gospel) are taught in the scriptures (Mosiah 1:3,5), by inspired men (Alma 12:9; Mosiah 2:9), and through the Holy Ghost (1 Nephi 10:19).

EVENT 2: Benjamin Confers the Kingdom upon Mosiah (Mosiah 1:9–18)

Benjamin grew old. Knowing he would soon die, he told his son Mosiah to tell the people to gather at the temple the next day, when he would tell them that Mosiah was to be their new king and ruler. Mosiah did as he was asked and told everyone to assemble at the temple to hear his father speak.

EVENT 3: Assembly at the Temple (Mosiah 2:5–8)

When the people came to the temple, they placed their tents with every family in its own area. They pitched their tent doors facing the temple so they could stay in their tents and still hear what Benjamin was going to say. Unable to teach the large number of people inside the temple walls, Benjamin had a tower built so the people could hear him. For those who still could not hear him, his words were written and sent to them.

EVENT 4: Benjamin's Address (Mosiah 2:17–4:30)

- Benjamin taught the people that service to others is the same as service to God (2:17). He said that even if they served God with their whole souls, they would not be able to pay Him back for everything He has done for them (2:21).

- All God wanted them to do is to keep His commandments, and if they kept the commandments, they would prosper (2:22). God had created them and given them their lives, and they could never pay Him back for that (2:23–24).

- If they refused to obey the commandments after having been taught them, God's Spirit would leave them (2:36–37).

- People would be judged by the good or evil things they did (3:24). Benjamin described two different conditions of the people:

1. Those who do not repent—who knowingly transgress God's laws and withdraw themselves from the Lord's presence. They feel guilt, pain, and anguish, which are like "an unquenchable fire" (2:38), and their torment is "as a lake of fire and brimstone" (3:27).

2. Those who keep God's commandments. They would be blessed in all things, both temporal and spiritual. If they were faithful to the end of their lives they would live with God in a state of eternal happiness (2:41).

EVENT 5: Benjamin Repeats an Angel's Prophecies about Jesus Christ and his Atonement (Mosiah 3)

An angel of the Lord had appeared to Benjamin and told him about the birth, life, mission, death, and resurrection of Jesus Christ.

- The Lord God would come to dwell among men in a mortal body and be the Savior (3:5–11).

- The Redeemer would be called Jesus Christ, the Son of God (3:8, 12, 18).

- The Redeemer would bleed from every pore (3:7).

- He is the Creator (3:8).

- He would be crucified (3:9).

- He would rise from death on the third day (3:10).

- His blood atones for the fall of Adam and Eve. Christ atones for those who did not know about God's commandments. Among those knowing God's commandments who sin, only those who repent and have faith in Jesus Christ will be saved (3:11).

- Nothing would save man if it were not for the Lord's Atonement (3:15).

- His blood atones for the mistakes of little children (3:16) .

- Salvation comes only through Jesus Christ (3:17).

According to the angel, the following will be saved through the Atonement of Jesus Christ:

- Those who ignorantly sin (3:11),

- Those who have knowingly sinned, but who repent and exercise faith in Christ (3:12–13),

- Little children who die (3:16, 18, 21).

EVENT 6: Benjamin Teaches the People How to Live Christlike Lives (Mosiah 4:13–30)

Christ's Atonement raises individuals from being lower than "the dust of the earth" to being Christ's children. Christ rescues people from their lowly state (4:2; 5:7).

- Parents should not let their children go hungry or naked, break God's commandments, or fight and argue with each other, thus serving the devil. Teach children to do what is right, and to love and serve each other (4:14–15).

- Share with the poor. Do not say no to poor people who ask for your help, "These people have caused their own problems, so I will not help them, because they do not deserve it." Those refusing to help need to repent, because they will have no place in God's kingdom. We are all beggars. God gave us everything we have: our food, clothes, wealth, and everything we need. For those unable or have little to give but say in their hearts that they would give but cannot, because they have nothing, the Lord will bless them as though they have given (4:16–26).

- If you borrow something from a neighbor and do not return it when you said you would, you commit a sin. This may cause the neighbor to sin by becoming angry with you 4:28).

- Watch your thoughts, words, and deeds. Do not do more than you are able to do, but work hard and be wise. Benjamin could not tell the people about all the ways they could sin, because there are so many ways to sin that he could not count them all. They must always watch what they think, what they say, how they behave, and keep God's commandments (4:29–30).

OUTCOME: The People Experience a "Mighty Change" and Promise to Follow Benjamin's Instruction (Mosiah 5:1–2)

King Benjamin wanted to know if his people believed his words. All of the people answered with one voice that they believed everything King Benjamin told them. They knew it was true because the Spirit of the Lord caused a mighty change in their hearts, and they no longer desired to do evil, but to always do good.

15. Zeniff Battles the Lamanites (Mosiah 9–10)

MAIN CHARACTER

Zeniff—Father of King Noah, grandfather of King Limhi. Despite his being overly eager in wanting to regain from the Lamanites some of his ancestor's land, which led to poor decisions, he was a good and respected leader.

EVENT 1: The First Unsuccessful Attempt (Mosiah 9:1–2)

Zeniff had been taught the Nephite language and knew the Nephite land where his ancestors had settled. He was sent to spy on the Lamanites to see how they could be defeated. However, Zeniff saw all the good things they were doing and did not want them to be destroyed.

Zeniff returned to the Nephite camp and contended with the leader, because Zeniff wanted to make a treaty with the Lamanites. But the Nephite leader, a violent man, ordered Zeniff to be killed. Zeniff was saved because many also disagreed with the leader, and a battle broke out between fellow Nephites. Most of the men were killed in the battle.

EVENT 2: Zeniff Leads a Group of Nephites to Return to the Land of Nephi (Mosiah 9:3–10)

Zeniff was overly eager to go back and take all who wanted to go with him to reclaim their ancestors' land. For not remembering God as they should during their travel, they suffered hunger and afflictions.

Zeniff took four of his men to the king to ask the king if Zeniff and his people could live peacefully in their ancestors' land. The king agreed they could live there and told his people to leave those lands so Zeniff's people could have them. They built buildings, repaired the city's walls, raised crops, and began to prosper. However, the king secretly planned to place them in bondage.

EVENT 3: The Lamanites Attempt to Bring Zeniff's People into Bondage (Mosiah 9:11–19)

After Zeniff and his people had lived in their ancestors' land for 12 years, the king worried that Zenff's people would become too strong for the Lamanites to bring into bondage. The Lamanites were lazy. They wanted Zeniff's people in bondage to provide food so they could live without working. The king began to stir up his people to fight with Zeniff's people. A Lamanite army attacked Zeniff's people and began killing them. Those not killed ran to a Nephite city. Zeniff gave his people bows and arrows, swords, clubs, slings, and all kinds of weapons to fight the Lamanites. Zeniff's people prayed to the Lord for Him to save them. God heard and answered their prayers. Many Lamanites were killed, and the rest of them were driven out of the land.

EVENT 4: Prosperity and Preparations for War (Mosiah 10:1–5)

They began to have peace again. However, they made many weapons to be used if the Lamanites attacked them again. Guards were set up to protect against a Lamanite surprise attack. Peace and prosperity lasted for many years.

EVENT 5: War Again (Mosiah 10:6–10)

The Lamanite king died, and his son became the ruler. He stirred up his people to hate Zeniff's people. Zeniff sent spies to find out the Lamanite plans. The Lamanite armies came, wearing only leather skins around their hips and with shaven heads. Zeniff hid the women and children in the wilderness. All capable young and old men gathered to fight, were armed with weapons, and were put in groups according to their age.

EVENT 6: Lamanite Traditions (Mosiah 10:11–18)

The Lamanites knew nothing about the Lord's power. In addition to being strong men, they were rowdy, aggressive, and violent. Their ancestors had taught them to hate, murder, and steal from the Nephites.

OUTCOME: Nephite Victory (Mosiah 10:19–22)

To motivate the Nephites to fight with all their strength and put their trust in the Lord, Zeniff told his people how violent and wicked the Lamanites were. The motivation worked: they killed many Lamanites and drove out the survivors. Zeniff grew old and gave the kingdom to his son Noah.

16. Abinadi Prophesies (Mosiah 11–12, 15, 19)

MAIN CHARACTERS

Abinadi—a Nephite prophet who called King Noah and his people to repentance. He was the first Nephite in the Book of Mormon to die as a martyr by being burned to death.

Noah—a son of Zeniff, he became the Nephite king prior to his father's death. Unlike his father, he was very wicked. He was the father of Limhi. He died by being burned to death, just as Abinadi had foretold.

EVENT 1: Wicked King Noah (Mosiah 11:1–15)

Noah was not a good king like his father, Zeniff. He broke God's commandments and was not true to his wife. To support his riotous living, he made the people pay a 20 percent tax on everything they had. He replaced the good priests with bad ones. He had his people plant grapevines and build winepresses to make wine. He and his people soon became drunkards.

EVENT 2: The Prophet Abinadi (Mosiah 11:20–29)

Abinadi went among the people, saying that the Lord had seen their wickedness. Unless they repent, God will punish them. He will deliver them to their enemies, who will afflict them and bring them into bondage. Then when they pray for God's help, He will be slow to hear their prayers and will allow their enemies to continue to afflict them. After Abinadi told them these things, the people and King Noah became angry with him and wanted to kill him, but the Lord rescued him.

EVENT 3: Abinadi Returns (Mosiah 12:1–8)

Two years later, Abinadi came back in disguise so the Nephites did not recognize him. Abinadi told the people that the Lord had commanded him to tell them that they would be punished because they had hardened their hearts and had not repented of their wickedness. They would be brought into bondage. They would be killed, and vultures, dogs, and wild animals would eat their dead bodies. King Noah's life would be as worthless as a piece of clothing burned in a hot furnace.

EVENT 4: Abinadi Is Captured and Accused (Mosiah 12:9–16)

The people, angry with Abinadi, tied him up and took him to King Noah. They told the king that they had brought a man who had said evil things about his people and said that God would destroy them. He said that the king's life would be like a piece of clothing burned in a hot furnace if he did not repent.

EVENT 5: Abinadi's Trial (Mosiah 12:17–17:20)

King Noah had Abinadi put into prison (12:17), then brought before the king's wicked priests to be questioned. Abinadi answered their questions without fear. The king ordered Abinadi's death and declared him to be crazy (13:1).

EVENT 6: The Ten Commandments (Mosiah 12:33–13:24)

Abinadi cited the Ten Commandments which God gave to Moses on Mount Sinai.

10 Commandments	Where in the Book of Mormon?	Where in the Bible?
1. Do not have other gods.	Mosiah 12:34–35	Exodus 20:3 Deuteronomy 5:7
2. Do not make idols nor worship them.	Mosiah 12:36; 13:12–13	Exodus 20:4–6 Deuteronomy 5:8
3. Do not misuse God's name.	Mosiah 13:15	Exodus 20:7 Deuteronomy 5:11
4. Observe the Sabbath day by keeping it holy.	Mosiah 13:16–19	Exodus 20:8–11 Deuteronomy 5:12–15
5. Honor your father and mother.	Mosiah 13:20	Exodus 20:12 Deuteronomy 5:16
6. Do not murder.	Mosiah 13:21	Exodus 20:13 Deuteronomy 5:17
7. Do not commit adultery.	Mosiah 13:22	Exodus 20:14 Deuteronomy 5:18
8. Do not steal.	Mosiah 13:22	Exodus 20:15 Deuteronomy 5:19
9. Do not lie.	Mosiah 13:23	Exodus 20:16 Deuteronomy 5:20
10. Do not covet (seek to possess or own the belongings of others).	Mosiah 13:24	Exodus 20:17 Deuteronomy 5:21

EVENT 7: Abinadi's Teachings About Jesus Christ

Abinadi explained the following:

- God would make an atonement for mankind (13:28).

- Without the Atonement, which God would make, man would perish (13:28).

- No one can be saved without God's redemption (13:32).

- Moses prophesied that God would save His people (13:33).

- All the prophets have spoken more or less about these things; they have said that God would come down and take upon Him the form of man (13:33–34).

- God would come down among men and save His people (15:1).

- God would break the bands or chains of death (15:8).

- The Redeemer shall be called Christ (15:21).

Special note: Jesus Christ is referred to several times in the Book of Mormon as the Father (e.g., 15:1–4; Ether 3:14). How can Jesus Christ be known as the Father while Latter-day Saints and other Christians know Him as the Son of God? The words *Father* and *Son* are titles rather than personal names; thus they may be used to refer to more than one person. For example, you may be known as a son and a father or a daughter and a mother.

There are three ways in which Jesus Christ can be referred to as the Father (Ludlow 183–184):

1. He is the Father in the sense that He created this earth under the direction of His Father (15:4; 16:15; Alma 11:38–39; 3 Nephi 9:15: Ether 4:7).

2. He is the Father of all who accept the gospel and are "born again" through the Atonement (5:7–8; 15:10–13, 27:25–27; Ether 3).

3. He is the Father because His Father gave Him the power and authority to act for and represent Him on this earth.

EVENT 8: Abinadi Gives One of the Most Important Statements About Christ's Atonement
(Mosiah 15:8–9, 19–26)

God broke the chains of death and gained victory over it by giving His son the power to intercede on our behalf—to plead our cause through His mercy. The Savior is able to do this because He takes the sins of all people upon Himself, redeeming them, and thus satisfying the demands of justice (15:8–9).

Without Christ's salvation, which was planned before the beginning of the world, all people would die and never rise again (15:19). But the chains of death will be broken, and the Son has power over the dead, so He will bring the dead back to life (resurrected) (15:20).

Abinadi explained that God has provided two resurrections:

1. The first resurrection applies to (a) all the prophets, (b) those who believed in the prophets' words, (c) those who kept God's commandments, (d) those who were good people, but died before Christ came, and did not know about Christ and His salvation, and (e) little children who have died (15:21–25).

2. The second resurrection applies to the rebellious who die in their sins—all those who knew God's commandments but did not keep them (15:26–27).

EVENT 9: Alma Is Converted (Mosiah 17:2–4)

Among King Noah's priests was a young man named Alma. He believed Abinadi because he knew what Abinadi had said about their wickedness was true. He pleaded with the king to let Abinadi go away in peace. This made the king angrier. He had Alma thrown out and sent his servants after him to kill him. But Alma escaped and hid. While hiding for many days, he wrote everything Abinadi had said.

EVENT 10: Abinadi Is Condemned to Die (Mosiah 17:6–12)

Three days later after talking with his priests, the king told Abinadi they had found a reason to kill him because he had said that God would come down and live among the people. The king told Abinadi that unless he took back all the bad things he had said about him and his people, he would die (17:6–8). Abinadi answered that he would not recall what he had said, because what he said was true, and he was willing to die. If King Noah killed him, he would be killing an innocent person (17:9–10).

Influenced by Abinadi's testimony, the king almost released him for fear of God's judgment, but the priests appealed to the king's vanity by reminding him that Abinadi had insulted him (17:11–12). Then the king became angry again and ordered Abinadi to be killed.

EVENT 11: Abinadi Is Burned to Death (Mosiah 17:13–19)

Abinadi was tied up and his skin whipped with bundles of burning sticks. As the flames scorched him, he shouted that the executioners' descendants would destroy other believers in God. The executioners themselves would be scattered, afflicted with many diseases, hunted, and finally suffer death by fire. King Noah would also die by fire. After Abinadi had said these things he died by fire (12:3, 13:10, 17:18).

OUTCOME: Abinadi's Words Are Fulfilled (Mosiah 19:2–24)

Some of the Nephites opposed King Noah and threatened him. Among them was Gideon, a strong man and an enemy to the king, who drew his sword and began fighting the king. The king ran and climbed up on the tower near the temple. Gideon was going up the tower to kill him when the king saw the Lamanite army coming and cried out in great fear for Gideon not to kill him. King Noah said that the Lamanites were coming and would destroy them (19:2–7). Gideon did not kill him. King Noah and his followers ran from the Lamanites, but the Lamanites caught up and began killing them. The king told his men to leave their families and keep running (19:9–11).

Many of the men who would not leave their families were captured by the Lamanites. Those who stayed had their beautiful daughters beg the Lamanites not to kill them. The Lamanites had mercy on them because of the daughters' beauty (19:12–14). The Lamanites did not kill them but said they could live in the Nephite land on two conditions: (1) bring King Noah to the Lamanites and (2) pay half of everything they possessed and afterward pay a heavy tax every year (19:15).

Most of the men who had run away with the king were sorry. They wanted to go back and help their families and people (19:19). But the king ordered them to stay with him and not to return to their families. The men, now angry with the king, burned him to death, as Abinadi had prophesied (12:3; 13:10; 17:18; 19:20). They were going to kill the priests, too, but the priests escaped into the wilderness (19:21). Then the men went back to their families (19:20, 24).

17. Alma Teaches Abinadi's Message and Baptizes (Mosiah 18)

MAIN CHARACTER

Alma — Also known as Alma the Elder;

- Before repenting of his wickedness, he was one of King Noah's wicked priests.
- Converted by Abinadi, he begged for Abinadi's life but was cast out by Noah, who sent servants to kill him.
- A Nephite prophet with divine authority, he founded Christ's Church during his time.
- He was the father of Alma the Younger.

EVENT 1: Alma Repents and Secretly Teaches the People (Mosiah 18:1, 7)

Alma escaped and repented of his sins. He secretly taught the people what Abinadi had said. The believers gathered to hear Alma teach about repentance, salvation, and faith in the Lord.

EVENT 2: Baptisms (Mosiah 18:8–10, 16–28)

With authority from God (18:13; Alma 5:3), Alma baptized hundreds of people into Christ's church. He ordained priests to teach the people. He told the priests to teach repentance and faith in the Lord (18:16, 20).

Some of the things he said they should do:

- Call yourselves the people of God (18:8).
- Help others with their problems to make their problems easier (18:8).
- Mourn with those that mourn (18:9).

- Comfort those who need comforting (18:9).
- Stand as witnesses of God at all times, in all things, and in all places (18:9).
- Live these covenants until death (18:9).
- Serve God (18:10).
- Keep God's commandments (18:10).
- Do not argue with each other but have love for each other (18:21).
- Keep the Sabbath day holy (18:23).
- Give thanks to the Lord your God every day (18:23).
- Meet together as often as you can on one day of the week (18:25).
- Share what you have with each other. If you have a lot, share a lot. If you have just a little, share a little, and give to those who have nothing (18:27).

OUTCOME: Alma's People Flee (Mosiah 18:32–35; 19:1; 23:3–7, 13)

King Noah learned about Alma's church and its location, so he sent his servants to spy on them. On the day the people gathered to listen to the gospel, the king found out about them through his spies. The king accused Alma of trying to get the people to rebel against him, so he sent his army to destroy them.

The Lord warned Alma that King Noah's army was coming, so the people escaped into the wilderness where the king's army could not find them. After traveling for eight days they came to a very beautiful land with pure water, where they began working very hard to farm and build buildings. The people wanted Alma to be their king. But he declined and said that it was not wise to have a king unless they could always have good kings (23:1–8).

18. Limhi and His People Escape from Bondage
(Mosiah 7, 19–22)

MAIN CHARACTERS

Limhi—Nephite king, son of king Noah (the wicked king responsible for Abinadi's death) and the grandson of Zeniff. Some Limhi-related events are told twice in Mosiah 7–8 and 19–22.

Ammon—A strong and mighty man. He was appointed to lead 16 strong men to the location of Zeniff and their relatives, who had left years earlier.

Gideon—Nephite leader. He opposed King Noah. See Story 21.

EVENT 1: Noah's People Enslaved (Mosiah 19:15, 17, 26)

The Lamanites captured many of the Nephites who had not escaped with King Noah. These captured Nephites could keep their lands on two conditions: (1) they had to deliver King Noah to the Lamanites, and (2) they had to give up half of everything they owned and pay a tax on half of everything they acquired each year. Limhi did not want his father to die, but Limhi was a good man and knew about his father's wickedness. The people chose Limhi to be the new king. He promised the Lamanite king that his people would pay heavy yearly taxes if the Lamanite king promised not to kill them.

EVENT 2: The People Suffer (Mosiah 19:28; 20:1–10; 21:2–12)

The Lamanite king put guards around the land to keep Limhi's people from escaping. The guards were paid from Nephite taxes (19:28). After two years of peace, the Lamanites sought revenge because they thought that 24 of their daughters had been taken by Limhi's people (20:6–7). Limhi's people successfully drove the

Lamanites away (20:8–11). After the battle, Limhi's men found the Lamanite king injured among the dead. The king's men had run away so fast that he was left behind (20:12). Limhi's men bandaged his wounds and took him to Limhi, where he was asked why he had fought against Limhi's people (20:13–14). The king replied that Limhi's people had carried away his people's daughters. Limhi, knowing nothing about this, said that whoever had done it would die (20:15–16).

Gideon told Limhi that it must have been King Noah's priests hiding in the wilderness who had kidnapped the Lamanite women, and that he should tell the Lamanite king in order to make peace with them to prevent their attacking and killing Limhi's people. The Lamanite king, now understanding the truth, told Limhi's people to come with him without weapons to meet his armies and promised that his people would not kill them. The king spoke to his people, and when they saw Limhi's people without weapons, they had mercy on them and returned with their king peacefully to their own land (20:17–26).

After many days the Lamanites again became angry with the Nephites. They did not dare kill the Nephites, because of their king's promise to Limhi. They struck the faces of the Nephites and made them do hard work. Limhi's people complained to him and wanted to go to war against the Lamanites. Because of the people's many complaints, he allowed them to do so. But the Lamanites defeated them, caused them to retreat, and killed many of Limhi's people. Three times without success Limhi's people tried to drive the Lamanites out of their land. Humbled by their defeats, they prayed to God for help, but the Lord was slow to hear them because of their wickedness. Nevertheless, the Lord heard their prayers and began to soften the Lamanites' hearts, resulting in a lifting of the people's burdens. They began to prosper and no longer suffered hunger (21:2–16).

EVENT 3: Ammon and His Companions Are Discovered (Mosiah 21:23–24)

King Limhi and his guards, seeing Ammon and his brothers outside the city walls, thought they were King Noah's priests. He had them tied up and put into prison. Limhi would have had them killed if they had been Noah's priests. When he found out they were not, but were fellow Nephites, he was overjoyed.

EVENT 4: King Limhi Interviews Ammon (Mosiah 7:13–15)

King Limhi told Ammon that as Lamanite slaves, they were made to pay high taxes, which were difficult to pay. Limhi said that Ammon could help his people escape. His people would rather be Nephite slaves than pay taxes to the Lamanite king.

EVENT 5: King Limhi's Speech (Mosiah 7:17, 19–20, 33)

King Limhi gathered his people and told them that it was their wickedness that had put them in bondage. They should trust and serve God, who would free them from bondage.

OUTCOME: King Limhi's People Escape (Mosiah 22:1–16; 23:30)

Gideon spoke after no other person had suggested any viable plan. Gideon told Limhi that the Lamanite guards at the city's back wall path got drunk every night. He suggested that the people gather their animals together and escape during the night into the wilderness. Limhi sent extra wine to the Lamanite guards, who drank it freely and became very drunk. When the drunk Lamanite guards fell asleep, Limhi and his people, led by Ammon and others, escaped.

When the Lamanites found that Limhi's people were gone, an army was sent to capture and bring the people back. But after two days of chasing the Nephites, the Lamanite army not only lost the Nephites' trail, but also became lost themselves in the wilderness. Limhi's people had successfully escaped.

19. Alma and His People Escape from Bondage
(Mosiah 23:6–24:25)

MAIN CHARACTERS

Alma the Elder—See Story 17.

Amulon—Leader of King Noah's wicked priests (Mosiah 23:32). The Lamanite king made him king and ruler over Alma's people.

EVENT 1: Alma Refuses to be King (Mosiah 23:6–15; 20–22)

The people wanted Alma to be their king, but he told them that it is not wise to have a king. If kings could always be good men, then it would be good to have a king. He reminded them of the problems wicked King Noah had caused.

Alma's people began to prosper; however, the Lord sometimes tests people's patience and faith. Whoever trusts the Lord will be saved by Him.

EVENT 2: Alma's People Brought into Bondage (Mosiah 23:25–30)

While Alma's people were working in the fields, a Lamanite army entered the land. Frightened, the Nephites ran into the city for safety. Alma told them not to be afraid, but to remember that God would save them. They prayed for the Lord to soften the Lamanites' hearts so they would not be killed. The Lord did soften the Lamanites' hearts, and the Nephites gave themselves up to the Lamanites, who took over the land. These Lamanite armies had become lost while trying to capture King Limhi's people who had escaped (23:30). See Story 18.

EVENT 3: Lamanite Promise Broken (Mosiah 23:36–39)

The Lamanites promised Alma and his people that they would grant them their lives and liberty if they would show them how to get back to their homeland. After Alma showed them the way back to their land, the Lamanites broke their promise. They put guards all around the land to watch Alma and his people. The Lamanite king made Amulon the king and ruler over Alma's people, but Amulon was not allowed to do anything the Lamanite king did not want him to do.

EVENT 4: The People Are Forced to Work (Mosiah 24:9)

Amulon remembered that Alma had been one of King Noah's priests, and that Alma, who had believed Abinadi, had been chased out by the king. Though Amulon was under King Laman, he ruled over Alma's people and made them work by putting taskmasters over them.

EVENT 5: Prayers Answered (Mosiah 24:10–12, 14–17)

Alma's people were treated so badly that they began praying to God. Amulon ordered them to stop praying. He put guards over them with orders to kill anyone caught praying. Alma and his people now began to pray to God in silence. The Lord heard their prayers and strengthened them, making their work seem easier.

The Lord told the people to be cheerful because He would save them from bondage. He told Alma to lead the people, and He would go with them and save them from bondage.

OUTCOME: Alma's People Escape (Mosiah 24:18–25)

All night long, Alma and his people gathered their flocks and some of their grain. In the morning the Lord caused a deep sleep to come over the Lamanites while Alma and his people escaped into the wilderness. After traveling all day, they made camp, and thanked God for having mercy on them, for making their work easier, and for saving them from bondage. The next morning, the Lord told Alma to quickly get his people out of the area, because the Lamanites were chasing them. After traveling 12 days in the wilderness, they reached safety.

20. Alma the Younger Repents
(Mosiah 25:19; 26:8; 27:1–36)

MAIN CHARACTERS

Alma the Younger—

- Son of Alma, who, along with the four sons of King Mosiah, was known for his rebellion and efforts to hurt the church.
- An angel's visit changed his and Mosiah's son's lives, after which he became a zealous missionary.

*Sons of Mosiah—*The four sons of King Mosiah—Ammon, Aaron, Omner, and Himni— grouped together (Mosiah 27:34).

EVENT 1: Mosiah Forbids Persecution of Church members
(Mosiah 25:19; 26:8; 27:1–2)

King Mosiah allowed Alma to establish churches and to ordain priests and teachers for each church (25:19). Nonbelievers made trouble for church members, whose complaints reached King Mosiah. He proclaimed that nonbelievers could not persecute church members (27:1–2).

EVENT 2: The Five Young Men Try to Destroy the Church
(Mosiah 27:8, 10, 14)

Mosiah's four sons and one of Alma's sons, also named Alma, were nonbelievers. Alma the Younger was especially wicked. He spoke well and caused many people do wicked things and to leave the church.

The five young men secretly tried to destroy God's church and lead people away from the Lord. Alma the Elder had prayed that his son would learn the truth and repent.

EVENT 3: Alma the Younger and Mosiah's Sons Are Rebuked by an Angel (Mosiah 27:11–16)

As the five young men were secretly trying to destroy God's church, an angel of the Lord appeared. He spoke with a voice like thunder, causing the earth to shake beneath them. They were so astonished they fell to the ground. The angel asked Alma why he persecuted God's church. The angel said that the Lord had heard the people's and his father's prayers. Because of his father's faith, the Lord spared Alma and sent an angel to show him His power. Alma should stop trying to destroy the church.

EVENT 4: The Effects of the Angel's Visit (Mosiah 27:18–20)

The five young men fell down again because they had seen an angel, whose voice shook the earth. They knew that only God's power could make the ground shake as if it was going to shake apart.

Alma the Younger was so astonished and became so weak that he could not speak or move his hands. Mosiah's sons carried Alma to his father and told him everything that had happened. This made Alma the Elder happy, knowing that it had been done by God's power.

EVENT 5: Prayers for Alma's Recovery (Mosiah 27:21–23)

Alma the Elder gathered people so they could see what the Lord had done for his son and Mosiah's sons. Alma called the priests together to fast and pray for his son's recovery. After the priests fasted and prayed for two days and nights, Alma the Younger revived, stood up, and began to speak.

EVENT 6: Alma's Confession (Mosiah 27:24–25, 29–31)

Alma the Younger told the people that he had repented of his sins, had been born of the Spirit, and was now saved by the Lord. The Lord told him that everyone needs to be born again—changed from their wicked condition to being righteous—to be saved by God and become His children. Alma reported that he had been in the darkness. His soul had been afflicted with terrible pain, because he had rejected Christ the Lord. After he waded through misery, almost to death, the Lord's mercy brought him out of the awful chains of wickedness. He was now saved, and his soul was free from pain. He knew that Christ would come, and that Christ remembers every creature He created. Every knee will bow and every tongue will say that He is God.

OUTCOME: The Five Young Men Began to Teach (Mosiah 27:32, 35–36)

Alma the Younger and Mosiah's sons taught what they had seen and heard, even though nonbelievers persecuted and beat them. They worked very hard trying to repair the damage they had done to the church, confessing their sins, telling about what they had seen, and explaining the prophecies and scriptures to those wanting to hear. They helped many people learn about their Savior.

21. Nehor Teaches False Doctrine and Kills Gideon
(Alma 1:1–31)

MAIN CHARACTERS

Nehor—
- A Nephite apostate, he introduced priestcraft and established his own church.
- A large man known for his strength. During an argument, he killed Gideon.

Gideon—
- As an old man he was a teacher in the church and stood up to Nehor's false teachings.
- When younger, he was a Nephite military leader who fought against King Noah (Mosiah 19:4), was a captain to King Limhi (Mosiah 20:17–22), and devised a Nephite escape plan to deliver the people out of bondage (Mosiah 22:3–9; 25:16; Alma 1:8). See Story 18.

Alma the Younger—See Story 20.
- Son of Alma the Elder
- Chief judge, who presided over the trial and execution of Nehor
- Governor over the Nephites, and presiding officer over the church
- Writer of some of the Book of Mormon's most important doctrinal discourses

---

EVENT 1: False Teachings (Alma 1:3–6)

Nehor went among the people preaching *false* doctrines, that

- Priests and teachers should be popular, be paid by the people, and not have to work with their hands (1:3). The people supported Nehor with money, and he became proud, wore costly clothing, and started his own church (1:6).

- Everybody would be saved and should not be afraid because of their sins. They should be happy, because the Lord had created everyone, would save everyone, and everyone would live with God again (1:4). There is no need for repentance (15:15).

EVENT 2: Nehor Encounters Gideon (Alma 1:7–9)

On his way to preach to his followers, Nehor met Gideon, who was serving as a teacher in the church. Nehor, in order to lead more people away from the church, argued with Gideon, who successfully defended the church with God's words (1:7–8). Nehor became very angry. With his sword he killed Gideon, who was too old to defend himself (1:9).

EVENT 3: Nehor's Trial (Alma 1:10–14)

The people took Nehor to Alma to be judged. Nehor boldly defended himself. Alma condemned Nehor for two sins, in accordance with the laws of the land:

1. He had introduced priestcraft (preaching false doctrine to gain popularity and wealth) by trying to enforce it with the sword. Nehor was free to teach false doctrine, but he did not have the right to enforce it (1:12).

2. He killed Gideon, a righteous man who had done much good (1:13).

EVENT 4: Nehor's Execution and Confession

Nehor was taken to the top of a nearby hill and executed. Before dying he confessed that everything he had taught was wrong (1:15).

OUTCOME

Nehor's execution did not end his teachings, which spread throughout the land (1:16; 21:4; 1:6; 16:11; 24:28–29). Moroni prophesied that priestcraft would be prevalent in the last days (Mormon 8:31–40).

The Lord prospered the faithful church members, even when they were persecuted. We can keep the commandments even when people around us are disobedient (1:28). In their prosperity, the faithful church members were not proud. They were generous to the poor, the needy, the sick, and the afflicted (1:27–31).

22. Alma's People Defeat the Amlicites
(Alma 2:1–3:19)

MAIN CHARACTERS

Amlici—Nephite rebel, follower of Nehor's apostate religion, who wanted to be the Nephite king. He was very smart and very devious; many people followed him (Alma 2:1–2).

Alma the Younger—See Story 20.

EVENT 1: Concern about Religious Freedom (Alma 2:1, 4)

A very cunning man named Amlici began to cause contention. Church members and others who did not follow Amlici became concerned that if Amlici became king, their right to worship would be taken away. The wicked Amlici wanted to destroy the church.

EVENT 2: Amlici's Unsuccessful Attempt to Be Elected King (Alma 2:3–7)

The people, whose right it was to determine who ruled as the king (2:3), assembled from all parts of the land into separate groups, some for and some against Amlici, arguing with each other before voting. The majority of the people voted against Amlici, who was rejected from becoming king (2:5–7).

EVENT 3: Amlici Gathers His Followers (Alma 2:8–13)

Not content with the peoples' decision, Amlici gathered his followers, called Amlicites, and provoked them to anger against those who had not voted for him. His followers made Amlici their king, who commanded them to arm themselves with weapons in an attempt to subject everyone to him. The Nephites, knowing what the Amlicites wanted to do, prepared to fight them by arming themselves with weapons and organizing themselves into different levels of leadership.

EVENT 4: The Amlicites and the Lamanites Join in Battle Against the Nephites (Alma 2:15–18)

The Amlicites attacked and at first killed many Nephites. However, the Lord strengthened the Nephites, who killed so many Amlicites that survivors ran away, being chased by the Nephites.

EVENT 5: The Nephites Defeat the Amlicites and the Lamanites (Alma 2:21–28)

Alma sent spies to follow the surviving Amlicites. The spies, very afraid, came running back into the camp. They reported that they followed the Amlicites and saw them join a large Lamanite army. The two armies together were destroying everything in their path while heading to attack their city. If they did not go quickly, their city would be taken and their families killed (2:21, 24–26).

Alma led the Nephite army back to their city, and as they were crossing a river, large numbers of the Lamanite and Amlicite armies attacked them.

The Lord, having heard the prayers of the Nephites, made them strong, even though they had fewer soldiers, and they began killing the Lamanites and Amlicites. Led by Alma, the Nephite army was able to head off and defeat the combined Lamanite and Amlicite army (2:27–28).

OUTCOME: Alma Victorious (Alma 2:29–38)

Alma and Amlici fought each other with swords. Alma prayed that his life would be saved and his people preserved. Alma was strengthened and killed Amlici (2:29–31). Alma also fought the Lamanite king, who ran away and sent his guards to fight Alma and his guards. The Lamanites were either killed or ran away. The Nephites chased the Lamanites and Amlicites into the wilderness, where many of the wounded died and were eaten by wild animals and vultures (2:36–38).

When we call upon God to help us stand against wickedness, He will strengthen us (2:28).

23. Zeezrom, a Wicked Lawyer, Converts to the Church (Alma 10:30–15:13)

MAIN CHARACTERS

Zeezrom—One of the most expert and cunning of lawyers. He later embraced Alma and Amulek's teachings.

Alma the Younger—See Story 20.

Amulek—Converted by Alma the Younger, he became his missionary companion.

EVENT 1: Alma Issues a Warning; Amulek's Testimony (Alma 9:12–34; 10:9–10)

Alma told the people to repent or God would destroy them. Jesus Christ would come and save those who repented, were baptized, and had faith in Him (9:12, 26–27). This angered the people (9:31–32). Amulek began preaching to the people, telling them about an angel he had seen who testified that Alma was a prophet of God and spoke the truth (9:34; 10:9–10).

EVENT 2: Devious Nephite Lawyers (Alma 11:20).

The lawyers were paid according to how much time they spent dealing with the law. This is why they stirred up all kinds of trouble and anger—so they would have more work, which resulted in more money.

EVENT 3: Zeezrom Questions Amulek and is Taught about Repentance (Alma 11:21–37)

Zeezrom tried to bribe Amulek with money to say there is no God (11:22). He also tried to twist Amulek's words and discredit his teachings about Jesus Christ, the Son of God, and the salvation of wicked people (11:26–37). Amulek rejected the bribe and accused Zeezrom of lying (11:25, 36). Amulek taught that Christ would not save people in their sins: "No unclean thing can enter the kingdom of heaven" (11:37).

EVENT 4: Amulek Teaches About the Resurrection (Alma 11:40–46)

- Christ will come into the world to save His people by taking on Himself their sins. He will only grant salvation and eternal life to those who believe in Him (11:40).
- Christ's death frees everyone from the death of their body (11:42).
- The spirit and body will be reunited again in their perfect form. All will be brought to stand before God, and will remember all their guilt (11:43).
- This restoration applies to everyone: all will be judged by their good or evil works (11:44).

The people were amazed, and Zeezrom began to tremble (11:46–12:1).

EVENT 5: Alma Answers Questions about the Resurrection and Judgment (Alma 12:8–24)

Zeezrom asked to know more about the resurrection and the judgment (12:8). Alma told about the Creation, the Fall, the plan of redemption and happiness, the priesthood, repentance, and many other doctrines (12:9–13:20). He explained the purpose of life while we are on this earth: this life is a time of probation or a test—a time to prepare to meet God, a time to prepare for the eternity that follows death and the resurrection (12:24).

EVENT 6: Zeezrom Defends Alma and Amulek and Is Cast Out (Alma 14:6–7)

Hearing the people use his own arguments to condemn Alma and Amulek, Zeezrom, knowing that he had lied in his debate with Amulek, was silenced by Amulek and Alma's responses. Realizing he could not join the other witnesses who accused Alma and Amulek, Zeezrom publicly admitted his guilt and defended Alma and Amulek. Accused of being possessed of the devil, he was spit upon and chased out of the city, along with others who believed what Alma and Amulek had said.

EVENT 7: Women and Children Are Killed; Alma and Amulek Are in Prison (Alma 14:8–29)

The wicked people gathered the women and children who believed or had been taught about God's words and threw them, along with their records and scriptures, into a fire. Alma and Amulek were forced to watch the women and children die. Amulek wanted to use God's power to save them, but Alma told him that the dying people would soon be with God, and the wicked people would be punished.

The chief judge slapped Alma and Amulek's faces and mocked them because they had not saved the burning women and children. The chief judge put them into prison. Other evil men came to the prison and abused Alma and Amulek, who were tied up with strong cords, received no food or water, had their clothes taken off, and were spit upon.

Alma and Amulek prayed and asked God to free them. God's power filled Alma and Amulek, and they broke the cords that held them. When the people saw this, they were so afraid of being killed that they fell down and could not get out of the prison. Then the earth shook and the prison walls broke in half and collapsed. The evil men who had abused Alma and Amulek were crushed to death by the falling walls. Alma and Amulek, protected by the Lord, were not hurt. When the people saw what happened and saw Alma and Amulek walking out of the collapsed prison, they became scared and ran away.

OUTCOME: Zeezrom Is Healed (Alma 15:1, 3–12)

After leaving the city, Alma and Amulek found those who had been thrown out because they believed Alma. They also found Zeezrom, who had a burning fever, caused by thinking that Alma and Amulek had been killed, for which he blamed himself. Zeezrom asked them to heal him. Through his faith and Alma's prayer, Zeezrom was miraculously healed (15:11). Alma baptized Zeezrom, who began to preaching to the people (15:12).

24. Ammon Serves as a Missionary
(Alma 17:18–23:7)

MAIN CHARACTERS

Ammon—One of Mosiah's four sons. Once numbered among the nonbelievers, he sought to secretly destroy the Church (Mosiah 27:8–10). He is visited by an angel and called to repentance. He and his brothers serve a 14-year mission (Mosiah 27:11–12). Do not confuse this Ammon with the one in Story 18.

Lamoni—A Lamanite king, a descendant of Ishmael, who was Ammon's first Lamanite convert.

Lamoni's wife—The queen and faithful wife who watched over her husband all night when others thought he was dead.

Abish—A Lamanite woman who was a servant to King Lamoni. She had been converted to Christ as a result of a vision her father received, but she had never told anyone about her beliefs. She is one of only five women mentioned by name in the Book of Mormon. The others are Sariah (1 Nephi 2:5), Eve (1 Nephi 5:11), Mary (Mosiah 3:8), and Isabel (Alma 39:3).

The Father of Lamoni—Unnamed in the Book of Mormon; king over all the Lamanites. He played a very significant part in allowing the gospel to be taught to the Lamanites.

EVENT 1: Ammon Becomes a Servant to King Lamoni
(Alma 17:13–25)

As a missionary, Ammon went among a "wild and a hardened and a ferocious people" (17:13–14). These people, the Lamanites, captured and tied him up. Any Nephite entering the area was always bound and taken to the king, who would decide whether to have the Nephite killed, made a slave, imprisoned, or thrown out of the land. Ammon told the king that he wanted to live among the Lamanites for a while, maybe until he died. Lamoni liked Ammon, had him untied, and wanted him to marry one of his daughters. Ammon refused, but offered to be a servant. He was assigned with other servants to watch over the king's flocks of animals.

EVENT 2: Ammon Defends the King's Flocks
(Alma 17:26–38)

After being the king's servant for three days, Ammon and the other servants took the king's flocks to a watering place where some Lamanites scattered the king's flocks. The servants were scared, because King Lamoni had killed other servants for allowing his flocks to be scattered. Ammon eased their fears and persuaded them to gather their flocks back to the watering place. When the same Lamanites threatened to scatter the flocks again, Ammon told the servants to protect the flocks while he would contend with those who were trying to scatter them. Because there were many wicked Lamanites, they were not afraid of Ammon and thought any one of them could easily kill him. But God's power was with Ammon. Ammon killed six of them by throwing stones with his sling. With his sword, he killed the leader, used it to cut off many arms, and chased the survivors away so the king's flocks could be watered.

Special note: Ammon cutting off arms may refer to him taking away the Lamanites' weapons and not to amputating human body arms. In the Book of Mormon, the most common use of the word *arm* is as a weapon (e.g., swords and clubs) (Gaskill 196–205).

EVENT 3: Ammon Teaches the Gospel to King Lamoni
(Alma 17:39–18:39)

After watering their flocks of animals, the servants herded the flocks back to the king, while carrying to the king all the arms Ammon had cut off. They told the king what Ammon had done. King Lamoni asked Ammon if he was the Great Spirit, to which

Ammon answered that he was not. Ammon then taught Lamoni about God, the Creation, Adam, the Fall, and the plan of salvation. Ammon told about Laman and Lemuel's rebellions and related past religious history.

EVENT 4: King Lamoni Is Overcome (Alma 18:40–43)

Lamoni believed Ammon and began praying to the Lord for mercy on him and his people. After praying, he fell to the ground as if dead. His servants carried him to his wife and laid him on a bed, while his wife and family mourned over him.

EVENT 5: The Queen Sends for Ammon (Alma 19:1–13)

After two days and nights, the servants were about to take Lamoni's body and put it in a tomb. Lamoni's wife, having heard of Ammon's reputation, sent for him. She told him that she did not think her husband was dead. Ammon told the queen that he was not dead, and tomorrow he would awaken, so he should not be buried. She believed Ammon and watched over the king all night. The next day, Lamoni awoke and said he had seen Jesus Christ, who would save all people who believed on His name.

EVENT 6: The Queen, Ammon, and Servants Are Overcome (Alma 19:11–16)

The king and queen, now both overcome by the Spirit, collapsed. Ammon prayed to God in joy, while the king's servants prayed in fear. Then they all collapsed.

EVENT 7: Abish Summons the People (Alma 19:16–24)

The only one left standing was Abish, who had been converted to the Lord many years earlier because of a vision her father received. No one knew about her conversion. She ran from house to house telling the people what had happened.

A man whose brother had been killed by Ammon at the watering place drew his sword to kill Ammon but was struck dead.

EVENT 8: Recovery and Conversion (Alma 19:28–35)

Arguments among the people began over what had happened. It saddened Abish to witness the arguing. She raised the queen by the hand, and the queen stood on her feet and praised Jesus. The queen then took King Lamoni's hand, and he stood on his feet and began teaching them what Ammon had taught him. When Ammon awoke, he taught the people, as did Lamoni's servants, who said that their hearts had been changed, such that they did not want to do evil anymore. Many believed and were baptized, became a righteous people, and founded a church.

EVENT 9: Ammon and Lamoni Travel (Alma 20:1–7)

King Lamoni asked Ammon to go with him to meet his father. The Lord's voice warned Ammon not to meet Lamoni's father, who would try to kill him. Instead, he was told to go where his brother Aaron and two companions were in prison. King Lamoni traveled with him, because he said the king was a friend of his.

EVENT 10: Ammon and Lamoni Meet Lamoni's Father
(Alma 20:8–30)

On the way, they met Lamoni's father, who was king over all the land. Because his son had missed an important feast and was traveling with a Nephite, he was angry. In his anger, Lamoni's father commanded Lamoni to kill Ammon. But Lamoni refused. The older king drew his sword to kill his son, but Ammon stopped him by reasoning with the king that his son was an innocent man. The king then turned to kill Ammon, but Ammon withstood his blows and injured the king's arm so that he could not use it. Lamoni's father now begged for his own life. Ammon granted Lamoni's father life in return for his promise to let Ammon's brother and his companions out of prison. King Lamoni could retain his kingdom, and he would no longer be angry with Lamoni but allow Lamoni to do according to his own desires. The king granted what Ammon asked. He also wanted Ammon, his brother, and his companions to teach him. Lamoni and Ammon continued on to where they freed Ammon's brother and two companions from prison. Though having been ill-treated, they had been patient in their suffering.

OUTCOME: Lamoni's Father Converted
(Alma 22:2–27; 23:5–7)

After being released from prison, Ammon's brother, Aaron, and his companions went to Lamoni's father's house. They offered to be his servants, but the king said that he did not want them to be his servants. He insisted that they teach him. See the table for what Aaron taught.

Aaron's Teachings (Alma 22)

Creation	Fall	Christ's Atonement
22:10–11 God made everything in heaven and on earth.	22:12–13 Because of Adam and Eve's disobedience, they and their posterity were placed in a place influenced by pleasures and appetites.	22:13 The plan of salvation, arranged during the premortal existence, saves everyone who believes in Christ.
22:12 People were made to look like God.	22:14 People cannot save themselves.	22:14 The suffering and death of Christ atones (compensates or pays) for our sins, through faith and repentance.
		22:14 Christ would break the bands of death; the grave would have no victory (all people would be resurrected).

The king repented, prayed to God, and then collapsed as if dead. The king's servants ran and told the queen all that had happened. Thinking that her husband had been killed, she commanded her servants to kill Aaron and his companions. The servants refused, because they feared their power, so she told her servants to have the people come and kill them. Knowing the stubbornness of the people and fearing there would be a great disturbance among them, Aaron took the king's hand and helped him stand up. The king taught his household, who were converted to the Lord. He allowed Nephite missionaries freedom to teach anywhere.

Thousands gained knowledge of the Lord and were so greatly blessed that they never fell away, and they became a righteous people. They laid down their weapons and no longer fought against the Nephites (23:5–7).

25. Korihor Teaches False Doctrine (Alma 30:6–60)

MAIN CHARACTERS

Korihor—An anti-Christ who spoke against prophecies about Christ's coming.

Alma the Younger—See Story 20.

EVENT 1: Korihor, an Anti-Christ (Alma 30:6–20)

Korihor told the people that there would be no Christ (30:12). His other *false* teachings included that:

- No one can know the future (30:13).

- You cannot know about things you do not see (30:12–15).

- To believe you can have forgiveness of your sins (the atonement) is crazy (30:16).

- Smart people prosper, and strong people conquer (30:17).

- It does not matter what you do. Whatever anyone does is not a sin or crime (30:17).

- When you are dead, that is the end of life—there is no life after death (30:18).

- God has never been seen or known; He has never existed nor ever will exist (30:28).

The laws of the land protected Korihor's freedom of speech. People could only be punished for their crimes, not what they believed (30:7–11).

Ammon's people (converted Lamanites) tied Korihor up and took him to Ammon, their high priest, who had him expelled out of the land.

EVENT 2: Korihor Still Argues (Alma 30:21–30)

Korihor went to another city, and after preaching, he was tied up again and taken to the high priest and chief judge. When they saw how hard his heart was—that he would say terrible things even against God—they did not respond to what he said, but had him tied up and sent to Alma, who was the chief judge and governor over all the land. Korihor told Alma the same evil and wicked things he had said in other places.

EVENT 3: Korihor Versus Alma (Alma 30:30–55)

Korihor contended with Alma, implying that Alma wanted the people to join the church so Alma could live off the people and get rich. Alma reminded him that he did not get paid for preaching; he provided for his own needs by doing honest work.

When Alma asked Korihor if he believed there is a God. Korihor answered no.

Alma challenged Korihor by asking what evidence did he have that there is no God or that Christ will not come. Korihor replied to Alma that if he showed him a sign, he would admit there is a God, that He has power, and he would believe what Alma said.

Alma gave several evidences of God's existence:

• Testimonies of other people,

• Testimonies of prophets,

• The scriptures, and

• Observing God's creations—the earth and everything on it and how it and all the planets move.

OUTCOME: The End of Korihor (Alma 30:46–60)

Korihor still persisted that Alma show him a sign. Alma told Korihor that he was sad that he fought against the spirit of truth; it was better that his soul be lost than that Korihor bring many souls down to destruction by his lying and flattering words. Alma told Korihor that if he denied God's existence again, he would be struck dumb and be unable to speak again to deceive people. Korihor still persisted for a sign. So Alma told him that in the name of God, he could not speak anymore to deceive the people. Now Korihor could no longer speak. He wrote that he knew he could not speak and knew only God's power could do this to him. He said he always knew there was a God, but the devil tricked him. He asked for the curse to be taken away. Alma refused, because Korihor would only lead the people astray again.

The curse of being unable to talk did not leave Korihor. He was cast out and went from house to house, begging for food. What happened to Korihor was immediately published throughout the land; and it was declared that those who had believed Korihor quickly repent to avoid being punished in the same way. The people repented. Korihor's wanderings took him to another city, and as he went among the people, he was run over and trampled to death.

26. Alma Teaches How to Increase Faith
(Alma 32:27–43)

Faith is believing that something is true without actually seeing it (Alma 32:21).

> **The good seed** represents God's word (the gospel).
> **The heart** represents the receiver of spiritual impressions.
> **The fruit** from the tree represents eternal life.

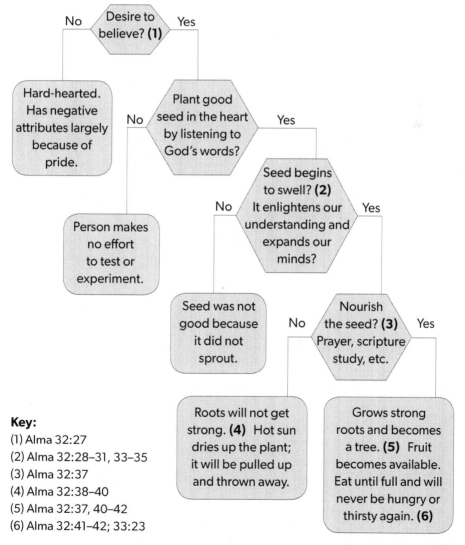

Key:
(1) Alma 32:27
(2) Alma 32:28–31, 33–35
(3) Alma 32:37
(4) Alma 32:38–40
(5) Alma 32:37, 40–42
(6) Alma 32:41–42; 33:23

27. The Plan of Salvation Is Explained (Alma 40–42)

God has a plan for us. It is known by several titles, such as "the plan of salvation" (Alma 42:5) and "the great plan of happiness" (Alma 42:8).

The plan of salvation teaches us where we came from, why we are here on earth, and where we will go after this life. It maps our eternal journey through pre-earth life, death, resurrection, and our life in the eternities. The plan focuses on the mission and Atonement of Jesus Christ in overcoming the effects of the Fall and making eternal life possible for us.

Although its teachings are not as complete as those found in latter-day scriptures, what the Book of Mormon teaches is in harmony with them. Latter-day scripture citations from the Doctrine and Covenants have been included below to reflect Latter-day Saint beliefs.

Two Major Divisions in the Post-Mortal World (Alma 40:12–14)

Everyone will rise from the dead (Alma 40:4). There is a time period between death and resurrection (40:6). A partial judgment at death determines one of two general destinations in the spirit world where people will stay until they are resurrected. The two places are:

1. Paradise—It designates a place of peace and happiness in the spirit world. It is reserved for:

   - Those who have been baptized and remained faithful Latter-day Saints while on earth (Alma 40:12; Moroni 10:34). These righteous spirits are called upon to teach the gospel as missionaries to those in the spirit world's prison.

   - Children dying before the age of accountability (Latter-day scripture, Doctrine and Covenants [D&C] 137:10)

   - Intellectually handicapped persons who are still childlike in their mental capabilities (D&C 29:50)

Some equate the word "paradise" with the word "heaven." The word paradise as used in the New Testament (Luke 23:43) is synonymous with the phrase "world of spirits." Latter-day scriptures teach that heaven is called the celestial kingdom (D&C 76:50–53, 70, 92).

2. Spirit Prison—It is a place where a wide range of people—good and evil—go. Good people are not being punished by being sent to the spirit prison, instead, they are given an opportunity to hear and accept the gospel of Jesus Christ, just as people on earth. If they accept it, repent of their sins, and accept temple ordinances (i.e., baptism) performed in their behalf, they will enter paradise before being resurrected. The same standard will be used to judge those who accepted the gospel of Jesus Christ in mortality (New Testament's 1 Peter 4:6; D&C 138:31–34, 57; 76:73).

Alma 40:13 calls the spirit prison "outer darkness." Some Latter-day Saints today view the term "outer darkness" as a description of the final destination of Satan, his angels, and sons of perdition (New Testament's Revelation 17:8, 11; D&C 29:36–38; 76:28–33).

Latter-day Saints view "hell" in at least two ways:

1. As another name for the spirit prison where those who were disobedient while on earth temporally dwell until the resurrection (D&C 138:32). It is not a place of everlasting torment (D&C 19:6–12).

All except the sons of perdition will be brought out and placed in a kingdom of glory, depending upon their level of obedience (D&C 88:21–24). This greatly differs from the belief that hell is a bottomless pit of eternal suffering and misery for all but the most righteous living on earth.

2. Known as the "outer darkness." After the resurrection and final judgment, it is for the devil, his angels, and sons of perdition (D&C 29:36–38; 76:28–33).

The first resurrection begins at the resurrection of Christ and includes the righteous who lived and died before His earthly ministry (Alma 40:16–21). Resurrection means the reuniting of the spirit and the body (Alma 40:21–23).

The following diagram shows the key points of God and Christ's plan for us. The Book of Mormon does not describe our pre-earth life nor the three kingdoms of glory. For additional information, go to these Latter-day scriptures—

- Premortal existence—Abraham 3:22–28; Moses 4:1–3

- Post mortal existence—Doctrine and Covenants 76; 131

Only our poor decisions can prevent us from enjoying the happiness found in God's plan of salvation.

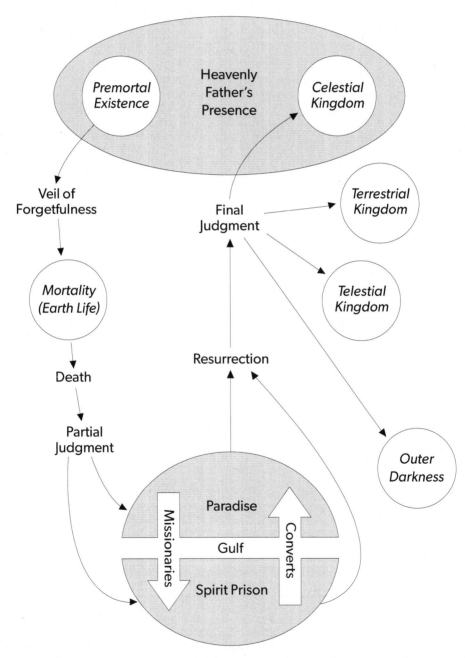

28. Moroni Defeats the Lamanites
(Alma 43:16–44:23)

MAIN CHARACTERS

Moroni (known as Captain Moroni)—Chief commander of all the
Nephite armies, appointed when he was 25 years old. Not to
be confused with the last author in the Book of Mormon, who
seals the record and witnesses the destruction of his people.

Zerahemnah—Lamanite military commander. His soldiers also
included rebellious Nephites.

EVENT 1: Moroni's Preparations Frustrate the Lamanites
(Alma 43:16–21)

The Nephites wanted to protect and preserve their lands, people,
and liberty. Moroni armed his people with swords and all kinds of
weapons. His soldiers wore armor to cover their chests, arms and
heads, and they wore thick clothing. The Lamanites were scared
of the Nephite armies because of their armor even though they
outnumbered the Nephites

EVENT 2: An Ambush Is Planned (Alma 43:22–33)

The Lamanites retreated into the wilderness with plans to make
a surprise attack elsewhere. Moroni sent spies to watch their
camp. He also sent some men to ask Alma to ask the Lord where
the Nephite army should go to defend themselves from the
Lamanites. The Lord told Alma, who told the men, who then told
Moroni that the Lamanite army was heading toward their weaker
defenses. Moroni sent out spies so that he would know when the
Lamanites were coming, and he divided his armies, placing them
in hidden positions.

EVENT 3: The Battle (Alma 43:34–54)

Lehi, who led part of the Nephite army, allowed the Lamanites to pass by him before attacking. The Nephites, despite being out-numbered, were able to kill more of the enemy because they were protected by the armor. So many Lamanites were killed that the remainder fled across a river, only to be met by Moroni's army. This time the Lamanites fought as they had never been known to fight, because of their anger. But the Nephites fought for a better reason—for their homes, liberties, families, and religion. Even though there were more than twice as many Lamanites as Nephites, the Nephites chased and surrounded them. When Zerahemnah's army found themselves surrounded by Moroni's army, they became terrified. When Moroni saw how scared the Lamanites were, he told his men to stop killing them.

EVENT 4: An Offer of Peace (Alma 44:1–7)

Moroni told Zerahemnah that they did not want to kill them or put them in bondage. He explained that the Lamanites were angry because of the Nephite religion: the Nephites had been victorious because of their faith in Christ. He commanded the Lamanites to give up their weapons and promise to never make war on them again.

OUTCOME: The Offer Is Rejected and Then Accepted (Alma 44:8–22)

The Lamanites gave up their weapons but refused to promise to never make war again—a promise they knew they would break. Moroni returned the weapons, because no promise was made. Moroni told Zerahemnah that they would end the conflict, because he could not take back the words he had said. He stated that Zerahemnah would not leave without making a promise to not return to war. Moroni added that they would kill Zerahemnah if he did not submit to the conditions offered.

In anger, Zerahemnah rushed toward Moroni with a sword, but one of Moroni's soldiers struck the sword, breaking it near the handle. Then the soldier struck Zerahemnah, cut off his scalp, showed the Lamanites the scalp on the tip of his sword, and said they would also fall if they did not give up their weapons and promise never to make war on the Nephites again.

Many obeyed and were allowed to leave, but Zerahemnah caused the rest of his men to become so angry that they chose to fight hard against the Nephites. Moroni was also angry because the Lamanites were so stubborn, so he told his soldiers to start killing those who had kept their swords. Because they were not protected by armor from the Nephite swords, many were quickly killed.

When Zerahemnah saw they were all going to be killed, he shouted to Moroni that if Moroni would not kill the rest of them, he and his people would promise never to make war on the Nephites again. Moroni took away the Lamanites' weapons and let them all depart into the wilderness. The dead were thrown into the river, which carried the bodies to the ocean.

29. Moroni Raises the Flag of Liberty
(Alma 46:1–37)

MAIN CHARACTERS

Moroni—Chief commander of the Nephite army. See Story 28.

Amalickiah—An apostate Nephite who became king of the Lamanites. He was a large and strong man.

EVENT 1: Amalickiah (Alma 46:1–10)

Many of the lower judges supported Amalickiah to become king when he promised to make them rulers over the people if they helped him become king. Because of his cunning and flattering words, many people left the church and sought to destroy God's church and liberty. His actions placed the Nephites in great danger.

EVENT 2: Title of the Liberty Flag (Alma 46:11–13)

When Moroni heard about the rebellions, he was angry with Amalickiah. He tore off a piece of his coat to make a flag, and on it wrote, "In memory of our God, our religion, our freedom, our peace, our wives, and our children." He tied the flag on the end of a pole and called it the "title of liberty."

EVENT 3: The Term *Christian* Used (Alma 46:13–16)

Dressed in armor, Moroni took the flag, bowed to the ground, and prayed to God that the blessings of liberty would continue as long as there were faithful believers in the land. Those who believed in Christ and belonged to the God's church were known as *Christians*.

EVENT 4: Moroni Chases Amalickiah and His Followers (Alma 46:19–33)

Moroni went among the people, waving the flag of liberty in the air and shouting for the people to support the cause of freedom. The people came running, wearing their armor. They promised to keep God's commandments and not be ashamed to be called Christians.

When Amalickiah saw that Moroni's people outnumbered his and that his followers were not sure that what they were doing was right, he took his faithful followers to join the Lamanites.

Moroni did not want the Lamanites to grow stronger and did not want Amalickiah to stir up the Lamanites. Moroni's army pursued and captured most of Amalickiah's army; however, Amalickiah with a few of his men fled and joined the Lamanites.

OUTCOME: Those Refusing to Take Loyalty Oath Killed (Alma 46:34–37)

Moroni had been given authority over the Nephite army by the chief judges, who in turn had been elected by the people. With this authority, Moroni had any Amalickiah follower put to death who would not promise to support the cause of freedom and maintain a free government. Only a few did not make that promise.

Moroni had the flag of liberty raised on every tower, and his people enjoyed peace again.

30. Amalickiah Becomes the Lamanite King by Deception (Alma 47:1–35)

> **MAIN CHARACTERS**
>
> *Amalickiah*—See Story 29.
>
> *Lehonti*—Leader of a dissident group of Lamanites who refused to obey the king's command to battle against the Nephites. He was made the king and leader over the dissenting group but was tricked by Amalickiah and killed by poisoning.

> **EVENT 1: Amalickiah Made a Commander** (Alma 47:1–4)
>
> Amalickiah and those who fled with him joined the Lamanites and stirred Lamanites to anger against the Nephites. The Lamanite king told his people to prepare to battle against the Nephites. When the Lamanites heard the order, they were afraid to displease the king, yet they also feared the Nephites, and so most decided not to fight the Nephites. This made the king very angry. He gave Amalickiah command of those who would fight and told him to force the other people to fight. This was exactly what Amalickiah wanted the Lamanite king to do, because he had an evil plan to take the king's throne and become king himself.

> **EVENT 2: Lehonti Is Poisoned, and thus Amalickiah Becomes the Lamanite Chief Commander** (Alma 47:6–19)
>
> The rebels chose Lehonti as their own king and leader and were determined not to fight the Nephites. They went to the top of a mountain to defend themselves. Amalickiah sent men up the mountain to ask Lehonti to come down and talk with him, but Lehonti didn't dare leave the mountain's protection to meet Amalickiah. On a fourth attempt, Amalickiah went near Lehonti's camp and told Lehonti to bring his guards with him. Lehonti

finally came down with his guards. Amalickiah told Lehonti that his plan allowed Lehonti's army to surround Amalickiah's army and take them prisoners if he, Amalickiah, would be made second in command. In the morning, Lehonti's army surrounded Amalickiah's army, which surrendered to Lehonti's men to avoid being killed. Amalickiah became second in command under Lehonti. Then Amalickiah had one of his servants secretly give small doses of poison to Lehonti until he died. The Lamanites then chose Amalickiah as their leader and chief commander.

EVENT 3: The Lamanite King Is Killed (Alma 47:20–29)

When Amalickiah returned with these armies to the Lamanite king, the king, who thought Amalickiah was returning victorious and had fulfilled his commands, went out to meet him. However, Amalickiah had his servants go forth to meet the king and bow low before him. When the king put forth his hand to raise them, a servant, acting on Amalickiah's orders, stabbed the king. Afraid, the king's own servants ran away, believing they would also be killed. Amalickiah's servants shouted that it was the king's servants who had killed the king and run away. The army pursued the king's servants unsuccessfully.

OUTCOME: Amalickiah Became the Lamanite King (Alma 47:32–35)

When the queen learned about her husband's death, she sent for Amalickiah and witnesses to testify about the king's death. He brought the same servant who had killed the king and others who were with him. They all testified that the king's own servants had killed him, offering as proof that they had run away. Amalickiah gained the queen's favor and married her.

31. King-men and Freemen Contend for Power
(Alma 51:2–37; 52:1–2)

MAIN CHARACTERS

Pahoran—A righteous judge who refused to be pressured by those with special interests

Moroni—The Nephite military commander. See Story 28.

Amalickiah—The Nephite apostate who wanted to be king. He led the Lamanites to battle against the Nephites.

Teancum—A Nephite military leader

Freemen—They wanted Pahoran to remain as chief judge, so they could keep their rights and their religion through a free government. They did not want to change the laws and be ruled by kings.

King-men—They were people from nobility who wanted to have kings so they could have more power and authority over the people.

EVENT 1: King-men and Freemen (Alma 51:1–8)

Some people wanted to change a few parts of the law. Pahoran, the chief judge, refused to change the law or even listen to those who tried to get him to change the law. Those wanting the law changed were angry with Pahoran and wanted him to give up his chief judge position. Arguing occurred, but no one was injured. Those wanting to get rid of Pahoran were called *King-men*, so a king could be the ruler rather than judges the people chose. Pahoran's supporters were called *Freemen* because they wanted religious freedom. A vote was taken, and the majority favored the Freemen, so Pahoran remained as the chief judge. Those wanting to have kings were descendants of nobility who wanted to be kings themselves.

EVENT 2: The Lamanites Prepare to Attack (Alma 51:9–11)

This was a critical time for the Nephites to have internal contentions, because Amalickiah was stirring up the Lamanites' anger against the Nephites. He was gathering soldiers and arming them with weapons, because he had taken an oath to drink Moroni's blood. Despite having a smaller army than before—the Nephites had killed thousands of his men—he gathered a large army and was not afraid to invade the Nephite land.

EVENT 3: The King-men Are Compelled to Fight
(Alma 51:13–21)

When the King-men heard that the Lamanites were coming to fight them, they were glad because they were so upset with the chief judge and the Freemen. They refused to take up weapons to defend their country's freedoms.

Their stubbornness angered Moroni against the King-men, because he had worked hard to preserve their liberty. Moroni wanted to stop the internal disputes and rebellion among the Nephites, because these had destroyed the Nephites in the past. Moroni received authority from the people to force the King-men to defend their country or be put to death. Moroni's army killed 4,000 King-men and imprisoned surviving leaders for later trials (there was no time to judge them then). Other King-men agreed to defend their country rather than be killed. That is how Moroni put an end to the King-men.

EVENT 4: The Lamanite Invasion (Alma 51:22–27)

While Moroni was dealing with the internal problems the King-men had caused, and while preparing to battle the Lamanites, the Lamanites invaded. Amalickiah took over many cities and fortifications. Moroni had previously made the conquered cities very strong, and now the King-men occupied these cities.

OUTCOME: Teancum Kills Amalickiah (Alma 51:31–52:2)

The Lamanite army was stopped by Teancum's men, who were stronger and better soldiers than any of the Lamanites. The Nephites killed many Lamanites until it got dark. When night came, both of the opposing armies stopped fighting and camped in separate locations. That night, Teancum and his servant secretly went into Amalickiah's camp. All were asleep because they were tired from fighting during the heat of the day. Teancum secretly went into Amalickiah's tent and put a spear into his heart. The king died instantly without waking anyone.

Teancum went back to his own camp, woke his men up, and told them what he had done. In the morning when the Lamanites woke up, found Amalickiah dead, and saw that Teancum and his men were ready to fight, they were so afraid that the Lamanite army retreated to a fort for protection.

32. 2,000 Young Warriors Are Victorious
(Alma 53, 56)

MAIN CHARACTERS

Helaman—The Nephite military leader of the 2,000 young warriors.

2,000 young warriors—Sons of converted Lamanites, known as the Ammonites, who had promised that they would never take up weapons again to kill others. These sons had not made the same promise their parents had made about killing. Another 60 young men of the converted Lamanites joined later (57:6).

Ammonites—A name given to Lamanites who had converted to the church through Ammon's efforts.

Antipus—A Nephite military leader killed in battle. His army was saved by the young warriors.

EVENT 1: The Ammonites' Oath Against Killing
(Alma 53:10–15)

Lamanites who had converted to Christ were known as *Ammonites*. They had settled among the Nephites, who had protected them against being killed by the Lamanites. The Ammonites had promised not to kill anymore. When they saw the danger and the many afflictions and hardships the Nephites had suffered to protect them, they were filled with compassion and wanted to take up their weapons and help defend their country. As they were about to break their promise, Helaman and others convinced them not to break it.

EVENT 2: 2,000 Young Men Make a Promise (Alma 53:16–22)

The Ammonites had many sons who had not made the same promise their parents had made about defending themselves against an enemy. The sons who were able gathered together and took up weapons. Two thousand young men promised to fight for liberty and to protect their people and their Nephite neighbors. The young men—courageous, strong, and trustworthy—became a great help to the Nephites. They asked Helaman to be their leader. They were serious-minded and had been taught to keep God's commandments.

EVENT 3: Helaman and the 2,000 Young Warriors Save Antipus's Army (Alma 56:28–50)

- Helaman and the 2,000 young men joined Antipus's Nephite army and were used as bait by marching in the open to entice the Lamanite army (56:28–33).

- The Lamanite army came out and pursued Helaman and his young warriors (56:35).

- While the young warriors were being chased by the Lamanites, Antipus's army came from behind and chased the Lamanite army (56:37).

- When the Lamanites saw Antipus's army coming behind them, they continued to try to overtake Helaman's group of young warriors, hoping to kill them before being surrounded (56:37). All three armies camped that night, none of them having over-taken the other (56:38). The chase continued the next day.

- On the second day, the 2,000 young soldiers marched as quickly as they could to avoid being killed by the Lamanite full-grown men (56:39–40).

- On the third morning, when the Lamanites stopped their pursuit, Helaman wondered whether it was a trap or whether Antipus's army had caught up with the Lamanites (56:43).

- He asked his very young soldiers if they wanted to fight the Lamanites (56:44).

- The young men had never fought, but they did not fear dying. They thought more of their families' liberty than they did of their own lives. Their mothers had taught them that if they did not doubt, God would save them (56:47).

- The Lamanite army had stopped, engaged in a terrible fight, and was beating Antipus's Nephite army (56:49–50).

- If Helaman and his young soldiers had not gone back to fight the Lamanites, the Nephite army would have lost (56:50). Antipus and many other leaders had already been killed (56:51).

- Helaman and his 2,000 young warriors arrived and began killing Lamanite soldiers (56:52). When Antipus's army saw that the Lamanites had turned around to fight the 2,000 young warriors, they attacked the rear of the Lamanites (56:53).

OUTCOME: Victory Without Any of the 2,000 Young Men Being Killed (Alma 56:54–56)

The Nephites—both Antipus's army and Helaman's army of young warriors—surrounded the Lamanites and killed many of them. The Lamanites were so terrified that they gave up their weapons and surrendered.

To Helaman's great joy, none of the young men were killed. It was a miracle that showed God's power.

33. Moroni and Pahoran Exchange Letters
(Alma 58–61)

MAIN CHARACTERS

Helaman — The Nephite military leader

Moroni — The chief commander of Nephite armies. See Story 28.

Pahoran — The Nephite chief judge

EVENT 1: Helaman Sends a Letter to Moroni for Help
(Alma 58:32, 34–36)

Helaman reported that his armies were too small to protect all the cities; he needed more men. He did not know why the government hadn't sent more help. If Moroni's army had not been successful and needed to keep the men, Helaman didn't want to complain. If that was not the case, then he felt there was something wrong in the government, because he knew more men could have been sent.

EVENT 2: Moroni Sends a Letter to Pahoran (Alma 59:1–3)

On receiving Helaman's letter, Moroni was happy to learn that Helaman and his people had regained their lands. He sent a letter to Pahoran asking him to send men to help Helaman's armies, so they could protect the land they had regained.

EVENT 3: Moroni Writes Another Letter to Pahoran
(Alma 59:13; 60:1, 5, 34–35)

A large Lamanite army that had previously been driven out by Helaman's army attacked a Nephite city that Helaman had taken back. They killed many Nephites. The surviving Nephites escaped and joined Moroni's army.

Moroni became angry with the government officials because they did not seem to care for the freedom of their country. He wrote another letter to Pahoran, pointing out that thousands of his people had been killed who might not have died if Pahoran had sent support as he should have. Moroni wanted to know why his people had been neglected for so long.

If Pahoran did not quickly send supplies and men, Moroni threatened to lead his army and take what his army needed.

EVENT 4: Pahoran's Replies to Moroni (Alma 61:1–18)

Soon after Moroni sent his letter to Pahoran, he received a letter back from him. He told Moroni that he was very sad that Moroni's armies were suffering. The reason for not responding was that many people had rebelled against Pahoran and tried to remove him as chief judge; they had forced him and his supporters to take refuge. After sending a proclamation calling people to arms, many in fact had gathered to defend their country and liberty, and to retaliate for wrongs done to them. So many had gathered, the rebels were afraid to battle them. The rebels had taken over the city, appointed a king to rule over them, and joined the Lamanites.

Pahoran told Moroni that he was not angry over Moroni's criticisms. He also wanted the Nephites to be free. He asked Moroni to bring a few men to help him, explaining that if Moroni gathered more men along the way, the combined army could defeat the Lamanites.

OUTCOME: Moroni Sends Help (Alma 62:1–10)

Moroni was happy that Pahoran was not a traitor to his country and still wanted liberty for the people.

Moroni took a small number of men to help Pahoran. He put up the flag of liberty everywhere he went, and thousands joined him. The combined armies of Moroni and Pahoran outnumbered the rebels (known as the King-men). When the armies fought, the rebel's leader was killed and his men became prisoners. Those who were captured and remained rebellious were quickly executed according to the law.

34. Hagoth Builds Ships to Move Thousands Northward (Alma 63:4–8)

MAIN CHARACTER

Hagoth — A Nephite who built ships for the Nephites migrating northward. He is described as being a very curious man.

EVENT 1: Nephites Expand to the North (Alma 63:4)

A large group of people—5,400 men with their families—left for the "northern lands."

EVENT 2: First Ship's Voyage (Alma 63:5–8)

Hagoth built a very large ship. Many Nephite men, women, and children departed on the ship with a considerable amount of supplies and sailed to the northern lands.

OUTCOME: The Migrants Were Never Heard of Again (Alma 63:7–8)

Hagoth built other ships. The first ship returned, and many more people with considerable supplies sailed for a second trip northward. They were never heard of again, and it was thought that they drowned in the sea. One other ship also sailed, never to be heard of again.

35. Gadianton Robbers Gain Power (Helaman 1–2; 6:19; 3 Nephi; 4 Nephi)

MAIN CHARACTERS

Kishkumen—A founder of secret combinations among the Nephites

Gadianton—The leader of the robber band formed by Kishkumen. He was known for his speaking skills, his secret murders, and his robberies.

Gadianton robbers—A wicked band originally led by Kishkumen, later by Gadianton and others. They unite to murder, rob, and gain power. They were successful because of their secret oaths and conspiracies. They are an example of a "secret combination."

EVENT 1: Conflict Over the Chief Judge Position; Pahoran Is Assassinated (Helaman 1:1–12)

After Pahoran died, his son, also named Pahoran, was elected by the people to be the new Nephite chief judge and ruler. Pahoran's brother, Paanchi, was angry. He wanted to be the chief judge and planned to lead his followers in rebellion, but he was captured and judged. The people determined that he should die for rebelling and trying to take away their liberty (1:5–8).

When Paanchi's angry supporters heard that he was condemned to die, they sent Kishkumen, who murdered Pahoran (1:9). Pahoran's servants chased him, but he ran so fast no one could catch him (1:10). Kishkumen and those who sent him all promised not tell anyone that Kishkumen had murdered Pahoran. Because of this promise and because he was in disguise when he killed Pahoran, Kishkumen was not suspected by the Nephites. Some of those who had planned to kill Pahoran were found and sentenced to death (1:12).

EVENT 2: Origins of the Gadianton Robbers
(Helaman 2:4–5; 6:18, 25–30)

Gadianton, a skilled speaker, killer, and robber, became leader of the group (2:4). From then until the end of Nephite history, such groups were named after Gadianton (6:18; 4 Nephi 1:42; Mormon 2:28).

Gadianton promised Kishkumen and his band positions of power and authority over the people if they made him chief judge. This is why Kishkumen wanted to kill Helaman (2:5).

EVENT 3: A Failed Assassination (Helaman 2:6–11)

One of Helaman's servants had been out at night, disguised as one of Gadianton's followers. He learned about the plan to kill Helaman, the chief judge. This disguised servant gave Kishkumen band's secret sign and gained the trust of Kishkumen, who asked the servant to take him to Helaman so he could kill him. As they were going to where Helaman was, the servant stabbed Kiskumen in the heart, and he died without making a sound. Then the servant ran and told Helaman everything that had happened, after which Helaman sent soldiers to catch the band of robbers and killers so they would be executed according to the law. When Kishkumen did not return, Gadianton feared for his life, so he and his band used a secret path to escape into the wilderness.

EVENT 4: Gadianton Robbers Destroy Peace
(Helaman 6:1–40)

The Lamanites became more righteous than the Nephites, who were now hardened, unrepentant, and wicked even though many Lamanites preached among them. It was a time of peace and prosperity (6:1–7). Then Satan stirred up the Nephites, so they joined with the Gadianton robbers (6:21–25).

EVENT 5: A Famine Humbles the Nephites (Helaman 11:1–21)

The wicked Gadianton band caused serious internal wars among the Nephites. Nephi, the prophet, prayed for a severe famine, which eventually humbled the Nephite people and brought them to repentance. The Lord caused rain to fall so their fruits and grain could grow again. This was then followed by peace and prosperity.

EVENT 6: The Resurgence of the Gadianton Robbers (Helaman 11:10–34)

For a brief time the repentant Nephites "swept away" the Gadianton robbers, who returned in a few years to cause trouble and destruction (11:10, 22–38). Later the Gadianton robbers became so powerful that they were able to resist the combined armies of both the Nephites and the Lamanites (11:32).

EVENT 7: War with the Gadianton Robbers (3 Nephi 2:11–19)

Several years after the birth of Christ, because of the Gadianton robbers' numbers and destruction, it necessitated that both the Nephites and Lamanites join to fight against them in a series of wars.

EVENT 8: Preparations for War (3 Nephi 3:1–4:27)

The Gadianton robbers' leader wrote a letter to the Nephite chief judge, demanding that the Nephites surrender and join them (3:1–10). The chief judge did not respond to the letter but instead enacted a plan to gather his people with everything they owned, including food, to one place (3:21–25). The robbers, who could no longer survive by stealing, were forced to come out in open battle and were defeated. Their leader was killed (4:1–7, 12–14, 26–27).

EVENT 9: The Reappearance of the Gadianton Robbers
(3 Nephi 6:28–30; 7:1–3).

Only a few years later, Gadianton robber practices resurfaced, resulting in the complete breakdown of the Nephite government (6:28–30; 7:1–3). The destruction of the wicked at the time of Christ's crucifixion eliminated the Gadianton robbers; but many years later, Gadianton's secret oaths and combinations began to recur (4 Nephi 1:42).

OUTCOME: Today's Secret Combinations (Helaman 6)

The Book of Mormon warns about secret combinations existing in the latter-days among all people of the earth with the specific goal to "overthrow the freedom of all lands, nations, and countries" (Ether 8:25). They will succeed unless those who know of the intent rise up against them (Ether 8:15–26). Characteristics of secret combinations include the following:

- The devil is the origin of such organizations (6:26–30).
- The Lord views such organizations as "above all the wickedness of the whole earth" (3 Nephi 9:9).
- These organizations thrive when most of the people are wicked and seek to benefit from the wickedness (6:21, 38).
- Secrecy marks such organizations (6:22, 25–26).
- These organizations involve taking an oath to keep any conspiracies secret (6:22, 25–26).
- The objectives for such organizations are to gain power or become financially rich, or both, so they can take over a nation (6:38; Ether 8:22). Moreover, they gain power and financial wealth with the active consent of the people, who "suffer these things to be" (Ether 8:23).
- These organizations use lies, immorality, money, and violence to achieve their ends (6:15, 17; Ether 8:10).
- The only way to limit such organizations once they are established and begin to thrive is by converting people to righteousness (6:37; 3 Nephi 5:4–6).

36. Nephi and Lehi Preach and Are Imprisoned
(Helaman 3–5)

MAIN CHARACTERS

Helaman—See Stories 32 and 33.

Nephi—Helaman's oldest son. His father taught him and his brother to be righteous. Nephi became the chief judge after Helaman's death. After resigning from the judgment-seat position, he and his brother Lehi preached the gospel full-time.

Lehi—Helaman's second son, who accompanied his brother Nephi on a full-time mission.

Note: Do not confuse Nephi and Lehi with others having the same name.

EVENT 1: Nephi Resigns from the Judgment-Seat Position
(Helaman 3:21–5:19)

Helaman had two sons, named Nephi and Lehi (3:21). When their father died, Nephi, the older son, became the Nephite chief judge (3:37). This time period was marked by internal and external strife (4:1).

Nephi, as the chief judge, saw the wickedness of his people and grew tired of it. The two brothers decided to go on a mission, hoping to cause their people to repent (5:4). Nephi gave up the judgment-seat position. After his preaching to the Nephite rebels, many confessed their sins, repented, and were baptized (5:17). Afterward, the missionaries went among the Lamanites. Blessed with the Lord's spirit, many Lamanites believed Nephi and Lehi and were baptized (5:19).

EVENT 2: Nephi and Lehi in Prison (Helaman 5:20–42)

While Nephi and Lehi were preaching, a Lamanite army captured them and put them into a prison, where they went many days without food. When their Lamanite captors went to the prison to kill them, they found the two men encircled by a protective pillar of fire. The Lamanites were afraid they would be burned if they touched them. Neither Nephi nor Lehi were burned, even though they appeared to be standing in the middle of the fire (5:21–23).

Nephi and Lehi told their captors not to be afraid: God showed them this marvelous thing so they would see that they could not kill them. The earth and prison walls shook, and a dark cloud covered the prison. Three times a voice from above called the Lamanites to repent and stop trying to kill Nephi and Lehi. Though the voice was mild, its power shook the earth and the prison walls. The Lamanites could not run away because of the dark cloud and were so scared that they could not move (5:26–34).

Through the dark cloud, a Nephite rebel and former church member saw Nephi's and Lehi's faces shining brightly as they talked with angels. When the Lamanites asked him how to get rid of the dark cloud, he told them to pray and repent until they had faith in Christ. They prayed to the Lord, until the dark cloud disappeared (5:35–42).

OUTCOME: Peace Is Restored (Helaman 5:43–51)

All the people were encircled with fire but were not burned. They were filled with happiness and the Holy Ghost and heard a voice proclaiming peace. The heavens opened, and angels came down and ministered to them. Most of the Lamanites, now converted, put away their weapons and gave the Nephites their land back.

37. Nephi Reveals a Murder and Is Accused of It
   (Helaman 7–9:38)

MAIN CHARACTER

Nephi—See Story 36.

EVENT 1: Nephi Reveals His Sadness and Preaches from a Tower (Helaman 7:3–8:26)

After being rejected for his preaching, Nephi returned to his home. Wickedness prevailed, and the Gadianton band came to control the government and occupy the judgment-seat positions. Seeing the wickedness of the people and feeling hopeless and sad, Nephi prayed out loud to God from his garden's tower, which was near a highway (7:10). Some men passing along the highway saw him in his garden tower and heard his sad prayer (7:11). They ran and told others what they had seen, and a large number of people gathered to know the cause of the sadness expressed for their wickedness.

Seeing from the tower the gathering of people, Nephi pointed out their sins and told them to repent or be destroyed (7:12–14, 17). Nephi said the Lamanites were more righteous than the Nephites because they had not sinned against the great knowledge the Nephites had been given. Therefore, the Lord would have mercy on them, would extend their lives, and would increase their posterity (7:24).

Corrupt judges, who were members of the Gadianton band, sought to turn the people against Nephi (8:1–4). However, many of the people supported him and what he said, so he continued preaching (8:11–26).

EVENT 2: Nephi Reveals the Murder of the Chief Judge; Five Men Are Sent to Confirm the Identity of the Murderer (Helaman 8:27–9:38)

Nephi told the people that the chief judge had been murdered by his brother, who wanted the judgment-seat for himself. He said that both brothers belonged to Gadianton's secret band (8:27–28).

Five men were sent running as fast as they could to see if Nephi was right (9:1–2). When they saw the chief judge lying dead in his blood, they fell to the earth, realizing that Nephi was a prophet (9:3–5). The chief judge had been secretly stabbed by his brother, who had fled in disguise. Being the first ones to discover the dead judge, the judge's servants had gone out to tell the people about the murder (9:6–7). The people were surprised to find the five men lying on the ground. They knew nothing about the others gathered in Nephi's garden. They were taken prisoner and blamed for the murder (9:8).

When the people gathered the next day for the chief judge's burial, the corrupt judges who had heard Nephi the previous day inquired about the five men whom they had sent (9:10–12). When the people brought the prisoners before the judges, they were questioned. After telling their story, the five men were cleared and released (9:13–15, 18, 38).

EVENT 3: Nephi Is Falsely Accused of Murder (Helaman 9:16–38)

The judges now blamed Nephi for the murder. Over the protests of the five men, Nephi was bound and brought before the judges (9:16–19), who offered Nephi money and would spare his life if he confessed to planning the judge's murder (9:20).

Nephi again told them to repent or be destroyed. He told them to go to the murdered man's brother and ask him if he killed his brother. The brother would first deny everything, act surprised, and say he is innocent. When confronted with blood on his clothing, he would turn pale, shake, and confess to the murder. The brother was found to act just as Nephi had said (9:22, 26–38).

OUTCOME: Nephi Is Set Free (Helaman 9:39–41)

Some of the people believed he was a prophet; others that he was a god, because only a god could know their thoughts and who murdered the chief judge.

38. Nephi Prays for a Famine to Humble the Nephites (Helaman 11)

This story is briefly described in Story 35 but is told in greater detail here.

MAIN CHARACTER

Nephi—See Story 36.

EVENT 1: Nephite Wickedness (Helaman 11:1–2)

The Nephites were fighting with one another throughout their lands. The Gadianton band were responsible for the destruction and wickedness.

EVENT 2: Nephi Prays for a Famine (Helaman 11:3–4)

Nephi asked God to send a famine in the land. He prayed that the Lord, would not let the people destroy themselves by the sword. Instead, Nephi asked that God let there be a famine to help them remember the Lord their God. Then perhaps they would repent and return to the Lord and righteousness.

EVENT 3: A Great Famine (Helaman 11:5–6)

A terrible famine occurred among all the Nephites. Even though the wars stopped, the famine went on and caused many deaths. No grain would grow because of the dry earth. The Lamanites as well as the Nephites were affected, and thousands died in the more wicked parts of the land.

EVENT 4: The People Repent; Nephi Asks God to Stop the Drought (Helaman 11:7–21)

When the people saw they were about to die of starvation, they began to remember the Lord their God. The people begged their leaders to tell Nephi that they knew he was a man of God—to ask him to pray to the Lord to stop the famine so they would not die. The leaders did what the people asked them to do. When Nephi saw that the people had repented and were humble, he prayed to the Lord again, saying the people were repenting. They had gotten rid of the Gadianton robbers completely and had buried their secret plans in the ground. Because of their humility, Nephi pleaded with the Lord to not be angry with them anymore, to please stop the drought and send rain so fruit and grain would grow again.

The Lord made the rain fall on the earth so fruits and grains could grow. All the people were happy and gave glory to God. They considered Nephi a great prophet, a man of God to whom God had given great power. The Nephites prospered, and there was peace.

EVENT 5: Wickedness and Pride Increase (Helaman 11:24–25)

Some Nephites who had joined the Lamanites began attacking the Nephites. They would kill and steal, then retreat to their secret places in the mountains and wilderness to hide so no one could find them.

OUTCOME: The Cyclical Pattern of Nephite History
(Helaman 12:1–6, 23)

We see how false and changeable people's hearts can be. The Lord blesses and prospers people when they trust Him. At the very same time people are being blessed with things for their happiness, they harden their hearts and forget the Lord because their prosperity makes their lives seem so easy.

Unless the Lord sends people afflictions, famine, and all other kinds of hardships or are hungry and thirsty, people do not remember Him. People are foolish and proud, quick to sin and slow to do good. People set their hearts on the worthless things of the world. They are quick to be proud, quick to boast, and slow to remember the Lord. They do not want the Lord to rule over them. Blessed are those who repent and listen to the Lord, for they will be saved.

See Story 39's diagram.

39. The Tragic Cycle Is Explained
(also known as the Pride Cycle)

This cycle is summarized in Helaman 12:2–6 and more detailed in Helaman 3–11; 3 Nephi 5–10.

In the Book of Mormon a tragic cycle (also known as the *Pride Cycle*) repeats itself many times: When God's people are righteous, they prosper. When they prosper, they become proud and forget God, the source of their blessings. When they become proud and forget the Lord, they fight, quarrel, make war, and commit all types of wickedness. This wickedness in turn leads to a collapse and destruction of nations. These calamities bring the people to repentance; they turn to the Lord in righteousness, and the cycle begins again. This same tragic cycle can also occur at the level of the individual. Keys to break out of the Tragic Cycle are found in Alma 13:28; 7:23; 62:44–51; Helaman 3:35; 3 Nephi 9:20).

Nephite Cycle of Righteousness
Mormon's Warning for Us Today

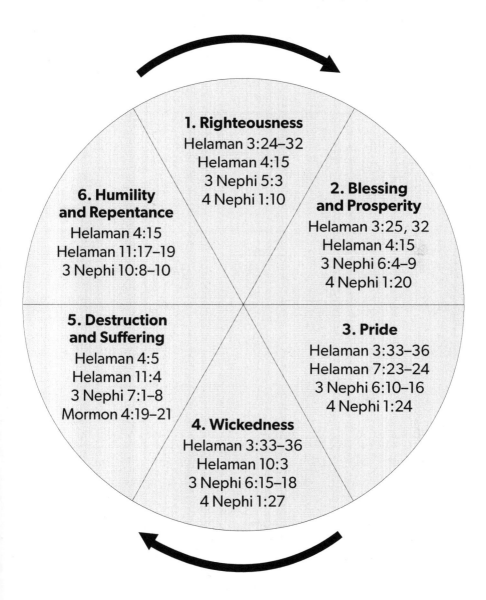

1. Righteousness
Helaman 3:24–32
Helaman 4:15
3 Nephi 5:3
4 Nephi 1:10

2. Blessing and Prosperity
Helaman 3:25, 32
Helaman 4:15
3 Nephi 6:4–9
4 Nephi 1:20

3. Pride
Helaman 3:33–36
Helaman 7:23–24
3 Nephi 6:10–16
4 Nephi 1:24

4. Wickedness
Helaman 3:33–36
Helaman 10:3
3 Nephi 6:15–18
4 Nephi 1:27

5. Destruction and Suffering
Helaman 4:5
Helaman 11:4
3 Nephi 7:1–8
Mormon 4:19–21

6. Humility and Repentance
Helaman 4:15
Helaman 11:17–19
3 Nephi 10:8–10

Source: John W. Welch and J. Gregory Welch (authors).

https://byustudies.byu.edu/charts/144-nephite-cycle-righteousness-mormons-warning-us-today

Courtesy of Brigham Young University.

40. Samuel the Lamanite Prophesies about Jesus Christ (Helaman 13–16)

MAIN CHARACTER

Samuel the Lamanite—The only Lamanite prophet found in the Book of Mormon. Except for his brief time preaching, nothing else is known about Samuel. Shortly before Christ's birth, he was sent among the wicked Nephites to preach repentance and the Lord's coming. At this time in the Book of Mormon era, the dominant pattern of Nephites being relatively righteous and the Lamanites being relatively unrighteous *was reversed*.

EVENT 1: Nephites Are Told to Repent; Samuel Is Rejected (Helaman 13:1–3)

The Nephites were wicked, while the Lamanites following the Law of Moses kept God's commandments. Samuel the Lamanite told the wicked Nephites to repent (13:2). The Nephites cast Samuel out. Because he had been rejected, Samuel was about to return to his own land, but the Lord's voice told him to go back and prophesy to the people the things that would come into his heart.

EVENT 2: Samuel Preaches from the City's Wall (Helaman 13:4–38)

The Nephites would not let Samuel back into the city, so he climbed upon the city's wall and preached from there (13:4).

- He prophesied that the Nephites would be destroyed in 400 years unless the people repented and had faith in Jesus Christ (13:5–6).
- The Lord did not destroy the city, because of a few righteous people in it. (13:12–14).
- Samuel said the Nephites were cursed because of their riches, and their riches were also cursed, because they loved them so much that they ignored the Lord's words (13:21).

- He told the people that they had tried to be happy by doing evil things, which is impossible, because evil is the opposite of righteousness (13:38).

EVENT 3: Four Truths to Know (Helaman 14:11–12)

Samuel gave four truths he wanted the people to know:

1. God's judgments because of sins

2. How to repent of sins

3. The coming of Jesus Christ who is the Son of God, the Father of heaven and earth, and the Creator of all things

4. The signs of Jesus Christ's coming

EVENT 4: The Need for a Savior; Three Types of Death (Helaman 14:16–19)

Samuel explains why it was necessary for the Savior to die: His death would bring about the resurrection, and it would save people from the first death, or spiritual death, and from physical death. Those who do not repent will be damned (the second spiritual death). Samuel describes three kinds of death, adding that Adam's fall brought spiritual death (separation from God's presence) to all people:

1. The physical death separates the spirit from the physical body and affects all people.

2. The first spiritual death automatically comes when we are born, as a consequence of Adam and Eve's Fall. We are separated from God's presence. All will be saved from this death and from physical death through Christ's Atonement and resurrection (14:15–19).

3. The second spiritual death occurs at the final judgment. When a person has not repented, he or she is banished from God's presence (Alma 42:9) and becomes dead to righteousness (14:18).

Three Kinds of Death

This table was adapted from an unknown source.

Physical Death	
Condition	• The spirit separates from the physical body. • Everyone will experience it. • It is temporary because of Jesus Christ's atonement and resurrection.
Cause	• The Fall of Adam and Eve brought physical death into the world. • It is caused by disease and injuries.
Cure	• It is unconditional to all people, through Jesus Christ's atonement and resurrection. • Everyone will be resurrected (the spirit reunited with the body). (Alma 40:23; see also Alma 11:41–45)
First Spiritual Death	
Condition	• It automatically comes upon all born into mortality (earth life). • They are cut off from God's presence or to things pertaining to righteousness (Alma 12:16, 32; 40:26) (Helaman 14:16–18) • It is temporary because of Jesus Christ's atonement and resurrection.
Cause	• There are two sources of spiritual death: 1. Adam and Eve's Fall (Helaman 14:16). 2. Our own disobedience and failure to keep God's commandments (Alma 12:12–16, 32; Helaman 14:18).

Cure	• It is conditional, because at the time of final judgment, those free from sin because of Jesus Christ's atonement and who have complied with God's laws will be rewarded according to their works.
	• Christ offers redemption from this spiritual death, but only if we have faith in Him, repent of our sins, and obey the principles and ordinances of the gospel. (Alma 13:27–30;)
Second Spiritual Death	
Condition	• At the time of the final judgment, those refusing to submit to Christ will suffer a second spiritual death. They will be cast out of the Lord's presence and will dwell with the devil and his followers (Alma 12:12–18, 32; 2 Nephi 9:16; Jacob 3:11; Alma 13:30; 40:26).
	• It is a permanent status.
Cause	• These individuals hate anything good and decent.
	• Those who have rebelled against the truth of the gospel will suffer a spiritual death, called the second death (Alma 12:16–18; Helaman 14:16–19).
	• It is the result of bad choices and rebellion against the truthfulness of the gospel.
Cure	• At the time of the final judgment, those who have lost the inclination or ability to repent or who commit the unpardonable sin are cast out into "outer darkness." (Alma 12:12–8, 32, 2 Nephi 9:16; Jacob 3:11; Alma 13:30; 40:26).
	• This second spiritual death could have been avoided through Jesus Christ's atonement if a person had repented. (Helaman 14:18–19)

EVENT 5: Signs About Jesus Christ (Helaman 14:2–7, 20–27)

Samuel made these prophecies about Jesus Christ's birth and death:

Prophecy	Events Related to Christ's Birth	Prophecy Fulfilled
Helaman 14:2	Christ to be born in five years	3 Nephi 1:13
Helaman 14:3-4	No darkness for a day, a night, and a day	3 Nephi 1:15
Helaman 14:5	New star appears	3 Nephi 1:21
Helaman 14:6	Many signs in heaven	Helaman 16:13; 3 Nephi 2:1
Helaman 14:7	People would fall to the ground	3 Nephi 1:16–17

Prophecy	Events Related to Christ's Death	Prophecy Fulfilled
Helaman 14:20, 27	Sun, moon, stars darkened for three days	3 Nephi 8:19–23
Helaman 14:21	Thunder and lightning for many hours	3 Nephi 8:6–7
Helaman 14:21-22	Earthquakes	3 Nephi 8:12, 17–18
Helaman 14:23	Great storms; mountains made low and valleys become mountains	3 Nephi 8:5–6
Helaman 14:24	Highways destroyed and cities abandoned	3 Nephi 8:8-11, 13–14
Helaman 14:25	Graves open, and resurrected Saints minister to people	3 Nephi 23:9–13

> ## EVENT 6: Samuel's Promises (Helaman 14:30–31; 15:7)
>
> Samuel said that those who die in their sins can only blame them-selves, because God gave them knowledge and the freedom to act for themselves—to know good from evil, and the freedom to choose life or death. You can do good and be given good, or you can do evil and be given evil.
>
> The scriptures can lead to increased faith, repentance, and a change of heart (Helaman 15:7).

> ## OUTCOME: Samuel Is Protected; Few Are Converted (Helaman 16:1–8)
>
> Some believed Samuel and went to Nephi, confessed their sins, and wanted to be baptized (16:1). Those who did not believe Samuel threw stones and shot arrows at him. But the Lord pro-tected him so they could not hit him (16:2). When the people saw he could not be hit, many more believed him and went to Nephi to be baptized (16:3). Nephi also taught the people about Jesus Christ (16:4–5).
>
> Most of the people did not believe Samuel. When they tried to capture him (16:6–7), he jumped off the wall and escaped to his own country, where he began to preach and prophesy (16:7). The Nephites never heard of him again (16:8).

41. Heavenly Signs Signify Jesus's Birth
(3 Nephi 1:1–26)

MAIN CHARACTERS

Nephi—Chief judge. Do not confuse this Nephi with previous individuals of the same name.

Jesus Christ—The second member of the Godhead and the only name by which salvation is given to the human family. He is the most significant person who lived or ever will live on this earth. Jesus's atoning sacrifice and resurrection exceed all earthly events, because He conquered death for all people and provided the only relief from the consequences of sin.

EVENT 1: Samuel's Prophecies Appear to Have Failed
(3 Nephi 1:5–9)

Some people claimed that Samuel the Lamanite's prophesies about the signs of Christ's birth were false because they had not yet happened. They began to persecute those who had believed him. The nonbelievers set a date for killing the believers unless Samuel's signs of Christ's birth came.

EVENT 2: Signs of Jesus's Birth Are Fulfilled (3 Nephi 1:10–21)

When Nephi heard about this wicked plan, he became very sorrowful. He bowed himself down and prayed to God all day. The Lord's voice told him to lift up his head and be cheerful, because the Savior was going to be born on earth the next day.

At sunset, there was no darkness. Many of the nonbelievers fell to the earth as if they were dead, because they had planned to kill everyone who believed the prophets. Instead, the signs had come, a new star was seen in the sky, and the birth of the Son of God would occur.

Special note: 3 Nephi 1:17 says that the signs of Jesus Christ's birth would be seen by "all the people upon the face of the whole earth." The whole earth referred to the Nephites' whole earth and therefore the signs were confined to a small region within Mesoamerica.

EVENT 3: Reactions to the Signs (3 Nephi 1:22–26)

Most of the people now believed in the Lord. Many repented of their sins and were baptized. Peace began to reign. There were no contentions, except a few who used the scriptures to try to prove that observing the law of Moses was no longer necessary. They were wrong, because they did not understand the scriptures. After being convinced that the law was not yet fulfilled, they confessed their mistake.

OUTCOME: Wickedness Increases, and the Gadianton Robbers Kill Many

• Signs of the Savior's birth happened just as Samuel said they would.

• But history repeated itself—the righteousness did not last long. About two years after the fulfillment of the prophecies regarding the birth of Christ, the numbers within the Gadianton robbers began to increase significantly, and they murdered many people (3 Nephi 1:27–30).

42. Signs of Jesus's Death Occur (3 Nephi 8–10)

MAIN CHARACTER

Jesus Christ—See Story 41.

EVENT 1: The Signs of Jesus's Death (3 Nephi 8:1–25)

Some people began viewing Samuel's prediction of three days of darkness as the sign of Christ's death. Others began to doubt and argue about it. Then the greatest storm ever known happened. In about three hours the land changed because of the storms, earthquakes, thunder and lightning. Many cities were destroyed.

When all these terrible things ceased, there was a thick darkness for three days. The darkness could be felt, and no candle, torch or other fire could be lit. There was no light from the sun, moon or stars. Great mourning, howling, and crying came from the survivors because of the darkness and destruction. In one place some wished they had repented so their families could have been saved.

Special note: Use of the number *three* in 3 Nephi 8:19, 23 cites *three hours* of destruction and darkness lasting for *three days*. The number *three* was often associated with divine things. It would have been difficult if not impossible to determine the hours because there were no clocks and impossible to differentiate day from night because of the darkness. Therefore, the number *three* is symbolic rather than an exact duration.

EVENT 2: The Voice of Jesus Christ Proclaims the Extent of the Destruction and His Mission (3 Nephi 9:1–22)

The voice of Jesus Christ was heard. Jesus told of the extent of the destruction, and many people were killed because of their wickedness. He proclaimed His divinity. He announced that the Law of Moses was fulfilled in Him, and no more sacrifices were necessary. Instead, the sacrifice was now a broken heart and a repentant spirit. He invited all to come unto Him to be baptized and receive the Holy Ghost.

EVENT 3: Jesus Christ Desires to Gather the House of Israel (3 Nephi 10:1–8)

After the people heard these things, there was silence in the land for many hours. The people were so amazed that they stopped mourning their dead family members. Then the voice of Christ was heard again. He promised to gather the house of Israel as a hen gathers her chicks under her wings for protection.

OUTCOME: The Reaction of the People (3 Nephi 10:8–19)

After three days, the darkness left and the earth stopped shaking. The surviving people thanked their Savior, Jesus Christ. The more righteous people had been saved from destruction. Mormon explained that these destructions had been prophesied (10:14–19).

Special note: The Second Coming of Christ will be similar to that described in 3 Nephi 8:19 and as found in 3 Nephi 9:1–12. Most people will not be ready for the Second Coming.

43. The Resurrected Jesus Appears to the Nephites
(3 Nephi 11)

MAIN CHARACTER

Jesus Christ—See Story 41.

EVENT 1: Heavenly Father's Voice Introduces Jesus, Who Appears to the Nephites (3 Nephi 11:1–17)

Many people gathered around the temple. As they were talking about the great and marvelous changes that had taken place and about Jesus Christ, they heard a voice from above, but they could not understand it. It was not a harsh or loud voice but a calm voice that went straight to their souls, causing them to shake and their hearts to burn.

Then they heard the voice a second time, but still did not understand it.

The voice came a third time, and this time they understood it: "Behold my Beloved Son, in whom I am well pleased, in whom I have glorified my name—hear him." Jesus then came down from above, clothed in a white robe, and stood in the midst of them. He said that He was Jesus Christ, and He had finished the work the Father had told Him to do. The people fell down, remembering that the prophets said Christ would visit them after He had gone up into heaven. Jesus told them to stand and come to Him so they could touch His side and feel the nail prints in His hands and feet. One by one, the people felt the wound marks.

EVENT 2: 12 Disciples Were Selected and Baptism Instructions Given (3 Nephi 11:18–28)

Jesus called Nephi and 11 others forward and gave them power to baptize the people after He, the Savior, returned to heaven. He instructed them in the correct procedure to follow and the words to say.

Jesus told them to go down, stand in the water, and speak these words after calling the person by name: *Having authority given me of Jesus Christ, I baptize you in the name of the Father, and of the Son, and of the Holy Ghost. Amen.*

Then, to put them completely under the water, followed by bringing the person up out of the water.

Special note: The baptismal prayer used in the Church today (see Doctrine and Covenants 20:73) is exactly the same as in the Book of Mormon (3 Nephi 11:25) with only one small exception—substitute the terms *having been commissioned* for *having authority.*

OUTCOME: The Doctrine of Jesus Christ (3 Nephi 11:28–41)

Jesus said that the Father told Him what to teach. Contention is not of the Lord, but is of the devil. The Savior's doctrine is that people must believe in Him, repent and be baptized, receive the Holy Ghost, and become as a little child. Those who believe, the Father will visit with the Holy Ghost, and the Holy Ghost will bear record of the Father and Christ. He promised that those who build their lives on His doctrine will be saved, and the devil will have no power over them.

44. Jesus Gives His First Sermon
(3 Nephi 12:1–18:39)

MAIN CHARACTER

Jesus Christ—See Story 41.

EVENT 1: The Beatitudes (3 Nephi 12:3–11; also Matthew 5:3–12)

Jesus gave the Beatitudes in a way similar to His Sermon on the Mount, with a few differences from Matthew's account in the New Testament. The statements start with "blessed are..." Four deal with us individually, and four with our relationships with other people.

Those dealing with ourselves *Blessed are those who . . .*	Those dealing with other people *Blessed are those who . . .*
Are humble	Are meek
Mourn	Have mercy on others
Want to be righteous	Are peacemakers
Have pure hearts	Are persecuted for following Christ

EVENT 2: How to Pray (3 Nephi 13:9–13)

Jesus gave the people an example of how to pray.
Special note: There are some very small differences between all three versions of the Lord's Prayer found in the New Testament's Matthew 6:9–13 and Luke 11:1–5 and the Book of Mormon's 3 Nephi 13:9–13. The Book of Mormon's prayer that follows is a direct quote. Just like the two New Testament versions, it is a model or pattern to follow:

Our Father who art in heaven, hallowed be thy name.
Thy will be done on earth as it is in heaven.
And forgive us our debts, as we forgive our debtors.
And lead us not into temptation, but deliver us from evil.
For thine is the kingdom, and the power, and the glory, forever. Amen.

EVENT 3: More Teachings (3 Nephi 12:13—16:20)

Jesus gave a sermon that parallels the New Testament version known as the Sermon on the Mount (see Matthew 5–7 in the New Testament). The message identifies a true disciple's behaviors and actions.

- Let your light shine before people so people will see your good works and give glory to your Heavenly Father (12:13–16).

- Christ came to make everything come true that the prophets have said (12:17–18).

- Come unto Christ and be saved. If you do not keep the commandments, you will not enter the kingdom of heaven (12:19–20).

- Do not murder. Whoever is angry with another person will be punished or whoever calls another person a bad name will be judged. If someone has something against you, go to that person and make things right again. Agree with your enemies quickly (12:21–25).

- To lust after a woman is committing adultery in your heart. It is better to deny yourself these things than to be cast into hell (12:27–30).

- If a man wants to divorce his wife, he must give her a divorce paper. If any man divorces his wife, unless she has committed sexual sin, he causes her to commit adultery (12:31–32).

- Do not swear (12:33–37).

- Do not fight evil with evil. Let whoever strikes you on the right cheek strike you on the left cheek, too (12:38–42).

- Love your enemies. Do good to those who hate you, and pray for those who do bad things to you and are mean to you (12:43–45).

- Be perfect as Christ is, or as perfect as your Heavenly Father is (12:48).

- Give to the poor, but do so in secret. Your Heavenly Father, who sees in secret, will bless you openly (13:1–4).

- When you pray, go into a place by yourself. Pray to your Heavenly Father in secret. Your Heavenly Father, who sees in secret, will bless you openly. When you pray, don't say the same things over and over. The Lord's Prayer is given as an example of prayer (13:5–13).

- If you forgive others, God will forgive you (13:14–15).

- When you fast, do so in secret. Your Heavenly Father, who sees in secret, will bless you openly (13:16–18).

- Do not work to get earthly riches. Work to get riches in heaven. Where your treasure is, there is your heart also (13:19–21).

- If your eye looks only for the glory of God, then your whole body will be filled with light (13:22–23).

- People cannot serve two masters. They will hate the one and love the other. You cannot serve both God and wealth (13:24).

- Seek first God's kingdom and his righteousness, and all these things will be added to you (13:33).

- Do not judge, or you will be judged. The way you judge others will be the way you yourself will be judged. Correct your own faults before trying to correct others' faults (14:1–5).

- Do not give holy things to the dogs, or things you love (pearls) to pigs (swine).

  Special note: In modern Western society, dogs are "man's best friend." In ancient Israelite culture, dogs represented an unworthy recipient of the gospel. Pigs represented anyone who would trample the word of God.

- Ask, and you will receive. Look, and you will find. Knock, and it will be opened to you. God knows how to give good things to those who ask Him (14:7–11).

  Special note: This is one of the most powerful promises ever given. It is the formula for getting personal revelation.

- Do unto others the things you want them to do to you (14:12).

  Special note: This statement is known as the "golden rule."

- Come in at the narrow gate. The gate leading to eternal life is very narrow, and very few people find it (14:13–14).

- Watch out for false prophets. You will know them by the things they do. A good tree cannot grow bad fruit, and a bad tree cannot grow good fruit (14:15–20).

- Not everyone who says "Lord, Lord" will get into God's kingdom. Only those who obey Heavenly Father will inherit His kingdom. Many will say they have done wonderful works in God's name, but God will say: "I never knew you, depart from me" (14:21–23).

- Whoever hears the things I say and does them is wise. But whoever hears what I say and does not do them is foolish (14:24–27).

- The Law of Moses is fulfilled in Christ. He gave Moses that law and made covenants with (promises to) the people of Israel (15:2–8).

- Christ is the law and the light. Have faith in Him and keep His commandments for the rest of your lives, and you will live forever (15:9–10).

- The Book of Mormon people are the "other sheep" whom Christ mentioned during His ministry in Palestine (15:12–24; see John 10:14–16).

- There are other sheep besides the Book of Mormon people who must be visited by Christ. (16:1–3).

- In the last days the remnant of the seed of these sheep will be gathered from throughout the earth. The truth will come to them through the Gentiles (16:4–7).

- In the last days, when the unbelieving Gentiles of this land sin against the gospel and will be filled with wickedness, the fullness of the gospel will come from among them (16:8–10).

- Then God will remember His covenant with Israel, and they will come to a knowledge of the fullness of the gospel (16:11–12).

- If the Gentiles repent and are numbered with Israel, God will not allow Israel to go among the Gentiles and walk all over them. If they do not repent, then Israel will go through and walk all over them (16:13–15).

- Then the words of Isaiah will come true: the Lord has comforted His people and has saved Jerusalem. All nations will see the saving power of God (16:17–20).

EVENT 4: Jesus Heals the Sick and Blesses the Children (3 Nephi 17)

Jesus had the people bring to Him their sick, and He healed them. He prayed for the people as they all knelt together. He blessed the little children. The heavens opened, and angels came down and ministered to the children.

EVENT 5: People Are Instructed on How to Pray (3 Nephi 18:18–25)

- Pray always to avoid the devil's temptations (18:18).

- Pray to the Father in Christ's name (18:19).

- Pray only for that which is right, believing that you will receive (18:20).

- Pray in your families so your family will be blessed (18:21).

- Pray in all your meetings and for others (18:23).

EVENT 6: Jesus Introduces the Sacrament (3 Nephi 18)

Jesus sent the 12 disciples to bring bread and wine to Him. When they returned, Jesus blessed the bread and wine (known as the *sacrament*) to His 12 disciples, after which He had them give the sacrament to the people. They were commanded to always follow the specific procedure and give the sacrament to all worthy Church members (18:6, 11). Jesus said that people who take the sacrament promise to always remember Him and His sacrifice. They then receive His spirit (18:7, 11). Those taking the sacrament promise to keep His commandments (18:10, 14). Those who eat and drink of His flesh and blood unworthily are damned (18:29). However, no one should be expelled out of the places where they worship; they should be helped, because they might yet repent and come unto Jesus (18:32). Jesus touched the disciples and gave them power to give the Holy Ghost (18:36–37). He then ascended to heaven. People gathered throughout the night to hear the Savior the next day (19:3).

Outcome: What Happens to Disciples of Christ (3 Nephi 12:13–16)

If we live according to the Savior's teachings, we will have a sure foundation and be strengthened to withstand whatever trials or temptations we may experience. We will become "the salt of the earth" and "the light of the people"; we will be able to help others draw nearer to the Savior.

45. Jesus Gives His Second Sermon
(3 Nephi 19–20, 23, 26)

MAIN CHARACTERS

Jesus Christ—See Story 41.

Gentiles—This label has several meanings: (1) in the Old
Testament and early parts of the Book of Mormon (e.g.,
1 Nephi), it describes nonbelievers or non-Jews; (2) in the
Book of Mormon it is not always easy to tell if the word
refers to non-Israelites or Israelites in a Gentile culture.

**EVENT 1: A Great Multitude of People Gather; the 12 Are
Baptized** (3 Nephi 19:5–34)

Because so many people had gathered, the disciples divided them
into 12 groups, and each disciple taught a group. The disciples
prayed for what they wanted most—that the Holy Ghost be given
them. The 12 disciples were baptized, beginning with Nephi, who
in turn baptized the other 11. They received the Holy Ghost and
were ministered to by angels. Jesus came, stood in the middle
of them, and blessed them. He prayed for them three times. His
words were so marvelous they could not be written or spoken by
people.

EVENT 2: The Sacrament Is Administered Again
(3 Nephi 20:1–9)

Jesus again administered the sacrament; the disciples and the
people had not brought any bread or wine with them, but Jesus
miraculously gave them bread to eat and wine to drink.

Special note: Defining a "miracle" is difficult. It includes events that
are largely unexplainable by known natural laws. In the gospel
sense, miracles are those supernatural events brought by divine
power which are beyond a human's power to duplicate.

EVENT 3: Jesus's Teachings on the Gathering of Israel in the Last Days (3 Nephi 20:10–22:17)

Special note: Throughout the history of the House of Israel, as the Israelites rejected God, they were scattered among the nations of the earth. Their prophets had warned of this scattering, but also prophesied that Israel would be gathered in the latter days. This gathering was to start as Israel came to a knowledge of the Lord (20:13).

3 Nephi 21:1–7, 9, 12, 22–29 contains one of the most significant statements about the gathering of Israel.

Jesus Christ taught that the coming forth of the Book of Mormon was a sign of the gathering of Israel in the last days (21:1–11). A man (Joseph Smith fits the description in these verses) will bring about this great and marvelous work of God (21:9–11).

EVENT 4: Jesus on the Words of Isaiah and the Importance of Samuel the Lamanite's Testimony (3 Nephi 23:6–13)

Jesus commanded the people to diligently search Isaiah's words, because Isaiah wrote important things. He talked about things happening to the House of Israel and to the Gentiles in his day, and also at the coming of Christ, and in the last days.

Jesus commanded that Samuel the Lamanite's testimony be written concerning the resurrection of many saints at the time of His resurrection (23:9–13).

OUTCOME: Jesus Explains All Things (3 Nephi 26)

Jesus explained everything from the beginning of the world until His second coming—everything that would happen, such as when intense heat would melt the earth, which would be wrapped like a roll of paper. All people will stand before God to be judged by their good or evil works. If their works were good, they would live again with God. If their works were evil, they would be damned. Mormon could not write even one percent of all the things Jesus taught the people. However, Nephi's plates contain most of the things Christ taught.

Jesus taught the people for three days, then later visited and taught them often. He ministered to their children, and the children spoke marvelous things to their fathers, even greater than what Jesus had said to the people.

The disciples taught and baptized from this time on. Those they baptized belonged to Christ's church.

46. Jesus Instructs the 12 Disciples (3 Nephi 27–28)

MAIN CHARACTER

Jesus Christ—See Story 41.

EVENT 1: The Lord Teaches the 12 Disciples and Names His Church (3 Nephi 27:1–12)

Because people were disagreeing on the Church's name, the 12 disciples asked Jesus what name should be given. Jesus said that everything they do should be done in His name; therefore, it should be named after Him because it is His Church. It could not be Christ's church if it is not named after Him. If you name a church after someone, then it is that person's church. If it is called after Jesus Christ's name, it is His church, so long as it is built on His gospel. Prayers to Heavenly Father should be done in Jesus Christ's name.

EVENT 2: The Gospel of Jesus Christ (3 Nephi 27:13–22)

Jesus came into the world to do what His Father sent him to do (27:13). The different parts or doctrines of the gospel are as follows:

- The Atonement (27:14)
- The resurrection (27:14–15)
- Judgment (27:14–15)
- Repentance (27:16, 19–20)
- Baptism (27:16, 20)
- Faith in Jesus Christ (27:19)
- The gift of the Holy Ghost (27:20)
- Enduring to the end (27:16–17, 19)

The Savior promised that those who lived according to His gospel would be blessed and lifted up at the last day (27:21–22).

Jesus asked His disciples, "What type of person should you be?" He then answered His own question, which was to be like Him (27:27).

Whatever you ask of the Father in Jesus Christ's name will be given you. Ask, and you will receive. Knock, and the door will be opened to you. Whoever asks, receives; and the door opens for whoever knocks (27:28–29).

EVENT 3: Jesus Grants the Individual Requests of the 12 Disciples (3 Nephi 28:1–12)

Jesus asked each of the 12 disciples what he would like from Him. Nine of them wanted to be with Him in His kingdom after a lengthy life on earth had ended. Jesus promised them that after reaching the age of 72, they would come to Him. The other three were afraid to ask for what they wanted, but Jesus knew their thoughts. They wanted to remain on earth, just like Jesus's apostle John (John 21:20–23 in the New Testament), and bring people to Christ until the end of the world.

EVENT 4: The Condition of the Three Nephite Disciples Who Wanted to Remain on Earth (3 Nephi 28)

The three Nephite disciples were changed into "translated beings," meaning that their bodies were changed so they could bring souls to Christ (28:9). They would:

- Never die but would live until Christ's Second Coming (28:7).
- Never feel the pain of death and would be changed in "the twinkling of an eye" (28:8).
- Never feel pain or sadness, except for the sinful conditions around them (28:9, 38).

- Not be subject to wicked mortal men, who would have no power over them; they could not be killed or harmed (28:19–22).

- Be able to show themselves to whomever they wanted (28:27–30).

- Preach, baptize, and give the gift of the Holy Ghost (28:23).

- Preach to "the scattered tribes of Israel," and to "all nations and people" (28:29).

- Have a change in their bodies so they would not experience death (28:37–39).

- Not be subject to the power of Satan, who could not tempt them (28:39).

- Remain in the changed body until Christ's judgment day (28:40).

OUTCOME: Jesus Instructed the 12 Disciples

- He gave the proper name for the Church (26:1–12).

- He preached gospel doctrines (3 Nephi 27:13–22).

- He promised that those living according to His gospel would be blessed and lifted up at the last day (3 Nephi 27:21–22).

- He taught that people should be Christlike in their actions and behaviors (27:27).

47. The Effects of Christ's Visit Last 200 Years
(4 Nephi)

EVENT 1: A New Society (4 Nephi 1:1–18)

Characteristics of the people:

- After Jesus Christ's appearance, all the people converted to Christ's church (1:2).
- There was no contention or fights because of the love of God which was in all the people's hearts (1:2, 4, 13, 15–18).
- All things were held in common—there were neither rich nor poor (1:3).
- Peace and prosperity prevailed in all the land (1:4–11).
- Church members fasted and met often to pray and hear the word of the Lord (1:12).
- There was complete unity (1:13–19).
- Contention and other iniquity disappeared—there could never be a happier people among God's people (1:13–16).
- There were no longer Lamanites, nor any kind of -*ites*. All were Christ's children, and all would live with God again (1:17).

EVENT 2: The Decline of Society: Apostasy Appears Gradually (4 Nephi 1:20–34)

- After 200 years without contention, a small group revolted against the Church and took upon themselves the name *Lamanite* (1:20–22).
- The people had become very prosperous because of Christ's blessings. Some of the people began to be proud, wearing expensive clothes and fine jewelry, and indulging in all kinds of other worldly behavior (1:23–24).

- They stopped sharing what they had with others. The people divided themselves into classes—some rich and some poor (1:25–26).

- The rebellious persecuted Christ's followers (1:27–34).

EVENT 3: The Downfall of Society: A Great Division
(4 Nephi 1:35–46)

- The people divided into *–ites* groups, and the number of such group names increased. The true believers in Christ were called Nephites, Jacobites, Josephites, and Zoramites. Those who did not believe in Christ's gospel were called Lamanites, Lemuelites, and Ishmaelites. These people were not wicked because of what their ancestors had taught them, they had chosen to be wicked and to fight against Christ and His church. They taught their children not to believe in Christ (1:35–38).

- Wickedness increased. Parents taught their children to hate. The wicked grew stronger, and there came to be many more of them than there were of God's people (1:39–41).

- The most wicked people became Gadianton robbers again. After 300 years, even the Nephites began to become proud and vain, just like the Lamanites, because of their extreme wealth. The only righteous people were Christ's disciples (1:42–46).

Summary of the Factors Ending the Long Era of Peace
(4 Nephi 1:20–46)

- Division and the creation of classes (1:20, 26,35).

- Pride and greed because of riches (1:23–25, 41, 43).

- Churches that professed to know Christ but denied most of His gospel (1:26–29, 34).

- Churches built up to help people get gain (1:26–29, 41).

- Hard-heartedness (1:31).

- Persecution of Christ's followers (1:29–34).

- Parents who taught their children not to believe in Christ (1:38).

- Parents who taught their children to hate (1:39).

- Secret combinations (1:42, 46).

OUTCOME:

- When people remained faithful to the gospel, "there could not be a happier people" (4 Nephi 1:16).

- After many years of peace, the majority of the people dwindled in unbelief and rejected the gospel.

- Ammaron hid the records so the rest of the House of Jacob would have them in the future, as God had promised (4 Nephi 1:47–49).

Special note: Jacob's name was changed to *Israel* (see Genesis 32:28 in the Old Testament); he was the father of 12 sons, whose descendants are known as the 12 Tribes of Israel.

48. Mormon Edits the Nephite Record and Sees His People Destroyed (Mormon 1–7)

MAIN CHARACTERS

Mormon—A Nephite prophet, army commander, and abridger of the Nephite records.

Ammaron—A Nephite who maintained the Nephite record and also hid all the Nephite records for safekeeping. He told 10-year-old Mormon to retrieve the records when he was about 24 and to continue adding to them.

EVENT 1: Mormon is Given Charge of the Records (Mormon 1:1–4)

Ammaron told the 10 year old Mormon that he had noticed him as a serious-minded child and quick to observe. When Mormon turned about 24 years old he was to:

- Go to the place where Ammaron had hidden all the Nephite records.

- Take Nephi's plates with him, leaving the other records there.

- Write on Nephi's plates everything he had seen happening to the Nephites.

EVENT 2: War Between the Nephites and Lamanites (Mormon 1:11–19)

The Nephite army defeated the Lamanites in many battles, killing many of the Lamanites. After the Lamanites retreated there was peace for about four years, but wickedness still existed. When Mormon turned 15 years old, the Lord visited him, because he was a serious-minded young man and knew of Jesus's goodness. He tried to preach to the people about Jesus, but was forbidden because of their wickedness. The Gadianton robbers lived among the Lamanites, and wickedness thrived. This condition fulfilled Abinadi's and Samuel's prophecies.

EVENT 3: War Continues (Mormon 2:1–26)

Mormon, even at age 15, was a very large man, and the Nephites made him the leader of their armies. He led the Nephite army against the Lamanites for many years. When a large Lamanite army arrived to fight, the Nephite army was afraid and would not fight. Mormon spoke to his men very strongly about fighting bravely to save their families and homes. Despite defeating the Lamanites, the Lord's power was not with the Nephites.

EVENT 4: Mormon Refuses to Lead His People (Mormon 3)

Mormon told the Nephites they would survive only if they repented, were baptized, and built the Lord's church again. But the people refused. After being victorious in battles, the Nephites bragged about their strength and swore retaliation for their companions who had been killed. Because of the Nephites' wickedness, Mormon refused to be their military commander. The Lord had told Mormon not to fight to get even; He, the Lord, would take care of "getting even."

Mormon records that all people would stand before Christ and be judged by Him, according to their good or bad works.

EVENT 5: Nephite and Lamanite Wars and Massacre of People (Mormon 4)

It was because the Nephites had attacked the Lamanites that the Nephites were defeated. God's judgment catches up with the wicked. He punishes the wicked by using other wicked people against them. After one battle, the Lamanites captured many Nephite women and children and sacrificed them to their false gods. This so angered the Nephites that they attacked and defeated the Lamanites. Eight years later, a large Lamanite army returned, and the Nephites suffered defeats and had to flee for their lives. Realizing that the Lamanites were going to win, Mormon retrieved the Nephite plates hidden by Ammaron.

EVENT 6: Mormon Leads the Nephites Again and Prophesies about the Lamanites and the Gentiles (Mormon 5)

Mormon told the Nephites he would help them, so they again made him the leader of their armies, thinking he could save them. But he had no hope for them, knowing that the Lord's judgments were upon them. They would not repent, but struggled for their lives without praying to the Lord. The Lamanites killed all the Nephites who had not gathered into the strongholds and burned their villages and cities. In desperation, the Nephites had to run for their lives. Those who ran faster than the Lamanites escaped; all others were killed.

Mormon wrote about the coming forth of the Nephite record (today known as the Book of Mormon) when the Lord saw fit. The book would go to the Jews to persuade them that Jesus is the Christ and that the Jews would be restored to their ancestors' land (5:14). The Lord reserved for the Lamanites the blessings He might give the Gentiles who would inherit the land. The Gentiles would scatter the Lamanites (5:19–20). Mormon warned the Gentiles to repent and recognize the power of God (5:22–24).

EVENT 7: The Last Battle (Mormon 6)

Mormon hid the records in the hill Cumorah, except those given to his son Moroni (6:6). The Nephites waited in fear of their final battle with the Lamanites, because of the size of the Lamanite army. All the Nephites were killed except 24, among them Mormon and his son Moroni. Mormon was wounded, a few

Nephites had escaped to the south lands, and a few had deserted and become Lamanites. Mormon mourned over his fallen people: had they kept God's commandments and not rejected Jesus, they would not have been destroyed.

Outcome: Mormon's Message to Latter-day Lamanites (Mormon 7)

Mormon admonishes the Lamanite posterity to repent, put down their weapons of war, and use them only if God commands them. He reminds them that as members of the House of Israel (7:1–4), they must come to the knowledge of their ancestors, repent, and believe that Christ has conquered death and brought to pass the resurrection of the dead (7:5–6). Those who repent of their sins and are not found guilty on judgment day will dwell in the presence of God in happiness forever (7:7).

The Nephite record (today known as the Book of Mormon) would invite them to believe the messages that would come to the Gentiles from the Jews (the Holy Bible); and if they believed the Holy Bible, they would believe in the Book of Mormon (7:8–9). If they believed in Christ, were baptized with water and then received the Holy Ghost, following the example of our Savior, it would be well with them on judgment day (7:10).

49. Moroni Finishes His Father's Book
(Mormon 8–9)

MAIN CHARACTER

Moroni — After the death of Mormon, his son Moroni wrote the last two chapters (Mormon 8 and 9) in his father's book, the "book of Mormon." Moroni was the only one left to write about the sad end of his people, the Nephites.

EVENT 1: The End of the Nephites (Mormon 8:1–11)

After the final battle at Cumorah, the Nephites who had escaped were hunted down and killed by the Lamanites. Moroni's father, Mormon, was also killed. Moroni alone survived to write the sad story of the Nephites' destruction. When he finished, he buried the records in the ground. The Lamanites continued fighting each other (8:8).

EVENT 2: Conditions During the Last Days When the Record (the Book of Mormon) Would Come Forth (Mormon 8:26–41)

- People will say there are no such things as miracles anymore (8:26).
- There will be secret combinations (e.g., gangs, drug cartels, mafia, terrorists, and other wicked organizations) (8:27).
- People will not believe in God's power (8:28).
- Churches will become polluted and proud. Church leaders and teachers will envy their own church members (8:28).
- There will be fires, smoke, and storms in many lands (8:29).
- There will be wars and rumors of war, as well as earthquakes (8:30).
- Much of the earth's air, land, and water will be filthy. There will be murders, robberies, lying, and sexual sin (8:31).

- Many people will say: "Do whatever you want, because the Lord will save you anyway" (8:31).

- Churches will say: "Give us your money and your sins will be forgiven" (8:32).

- People will love money, rich living, expensive clothes, and nice church buildings more than they "love the poor and the needy, the sick and the afflicted" (8:37).

- People will be ashamed to take upon themselves the name of Christ (8:38).

- People will do wicked things to get rich (8:40).

EVENT 3: Moroni's Message for Those Who Do Not Believe in Christ (Mormon 9:1–6)

Moroni asked if unbelievers would be able to stand in front of the Son of God and say there is no God and there is no Christ, even after they had seen Him. Moroni said they would much rather live with the damned souls in hell than live in shame with God.

EVENT 4: Moroni's Testimony of Miracles (Mormon 9:7–29)

Whoever says there are no more revelations, prophecies, healings, or spiritual gifts of God does not know Christ's gospel or understand the scriptures. The scriptures say that God is the same yesterday, today, and forever—He does not change (Mormon 9:7–9).

God does not do miracles if a person doesn't believe, doesn't keep the commandments, and doesn't know God in whom they should trust. Whoever believes in Christ, without doubting, can ask God the Father in Christ's name for anything, and they will get what they ask for. This promise extends to everyone (9:20–21).

Special note: See page 136, Event 2 for describing a "miracle."

EVENT 5: Moroni Summarizes the Plan of Salvation
(Mormon 9:11–14)

See Story 27 for more on the Plan of Salvation.

- God made heaven and earth and everything in them (9:11).

- He created Adam and Eve, who caused the Fall (9:12).

- Because of the Fall, God sent His son Jesus Christ to save (redeem) us from the Fall (9:12).

- Because of the salvation (redemption) of Jesus Christ, all people will obtain new bodies (be resurrected) (9:13).

- Jesus Christ will judge all people. Whoever is wicked will still be wicked, and whoever is righteous will still be righteous. Whoever is happy will still be happy, and whoever is unhappy will still be unhappy (9:14).

EVENT 6: Moroni Speaks About the Language of the Book of Mormon (Mormon 9:30–34)

Moroni counseled readers not to condemn him or his father or others because of mistakes in the writing of the records. They wrote on plates in characters called *Reformed Egyptian*, which they had been taught by Moroni's ancestors. If the plates had been larger, they would have written in Hebrew, which had changed over the years. God knows that no one else knows Reformed Egyptian characters, so He made a way for the characters to be understood and translated.

OUTCOME: Counsel to Latter-day Readers (Mormon 8–9)

- Moroni wrote about the sad end of his people, the Nephites (8:3).

- Most of Mormon chapters 8 and 9 were written for future readers of the Book of Mormon. Moroni said that whoever reads the book and does not reject it because of the mistakes in it will be able to learn even greater things than what is written (8:12).

- Moroni gave the following counsel to latter-day readers:

  –"Doubt not, but be believing" (9:27).

  –"Come unto the Lord with all your heart" (9:27).

  –"Strip yourselves of all uncleanness" (9:28).

  –Pray for the strength to "yield to no temptation" (9:28).

  –Do not be baptized unworthily (9:29).

  –Do not partake of the sacrament unworthily (9:29).

  –"Endure to the end" (9:29).

50. Jared's Brother Sees the Lord, and the Jaredites Cross the Ocean (Ether 1–3, 6)

MAIN CHARACTERS

Jared's Brother—This man's real name is never given in the Book of Mormon; he is only called "the brother of Jared." The Jaredites set up their tents by the sea and called the place Moriancumer (2:13). Traditionally, a location's name came from the name of the first person to inhabit it; thus it might indicate the name of Jared's brother. Joseph Smith said that Jared's brother's name was Mahonri Moriancumer. Jared's brother is described as a large and strong man, a man highly favored of the Lord (1:34), and known for his great faith (3:9).

Jared—Founder of the Jaredites

Jaredites—They were one of the three separate migrations to the ancient Americas in the Book of Mormon. Their history is found in the book of Ether. They were led by God from the Tower of Babel to the Western Hemisphere. They were destroyed by wars among themselves, the last survivor being Coriantumr.

EVENT 1: Jared and His Brother's Families Leave the Tower (Ether 1:33)

Building the Tower of Babel is reported in the Holy Bible (Old Testament's Genesis 11:1–9). The Lord, angry with the people who chose to build the Tower of Babel, confused their language so that they would not understand one another's speech. The Lord scattered them all over the earth. Jared departed from the Tower of Babel with his brother and their families, along with some other friends and their families (see also the Old Testament, Genesis 11:1–9).

EVENT 2: Jared and His Brother Appeal to the Lord (Ether 1:34–43)

Jared asked his brother to pray to the Lord that the language of their families and friends would not be changed, so that they could still understand each other, and to ask where the Lord wanted them to go.

EVENT 3: The Jaredites Begin Their Journey to the Promised Land (Ether 2:1–20)

The Lord wanted them to go to the promised land, a land better than all other lands, which He had saved for a righteous people. The Lord told Jared's brother that whoever possessed the promised land would have to serve Him or be destroyed (2:8). The warning and promise were for all people who would inhabit the promised land, not just the Jaredites (2:9–12).

When they arrived at the ocean, the Jaredites camped there for four years (2:13). After the four years, the Lord came in a cloud to Jared's brother and talked to him for three hours. He also told Jared's brother to repent, because he had forgotten to pray to the Lord. (2:14).

Jared's brother repented, prayed to the Lord, and began to build some barges. Following the Lord's directions, the barges were watertight (2:15–17), with no windows for air or light. Jared's brother asked the Lord how the people were to breathe and see while inside the barges. For breathing, Jared's brother was told to cut holes that could be opened or plugged up, one in the top and one in the bottom, to allow air into the barges. If water came in one hole, the other hole would allow the entry of air (2:19–20).

EVENT 4: Sixteen Stones (Ether 2:22–23, 25; 3:1–5)

For light in the barges, Jacob's brother was not given an answer. Instead, the Lord turned the problem back to him.

Jared's brother "did molten" (heated) 16 small stones (two stones for each of the eight barges) until they were like clear glass. Then he asked the Lord to touch the stones with His finger to give light during their journey.

EVENT 5: Jared's Brother Sees Jesus Christ (Ether 3:6–27)

As the Lord touched the stones one at a time with His finger, Jared's brother saw the Lord's finger, which looked just like that of a man. He was so afraid that he fell down. The Lord asked him why he had fallen. He replied that he had seen the Lord's finger and feared that he would be punished because he had not known that the Lord had a body of flesh and blood.

Because of Jared's brother's great faith, the Lord Jesus Christ showed Himself and explained that His premortal spirit body was the way His body would look when He came to live on earth, and that all people were made to look like Him (3:14–16).

The Lord showed him all the inhabitants of the earth who had lived and those who would live. He was told to write and seal up the things he had seen and not show them to anyone. The Lord would show them to all people in the future.

OUTCOME: The Jaredites Sail to the Promised Land (Ether 6:1–12)

Jared's brother put one stone in each end of the eight barges to give light during their travel. Animals, provisions, and people entered into the barges and asked God to protect them. A furious wind blew their barges toward the promised land. When they landed on the shore of the promised land, they bowed down and shed tears of happiness, thanking God for His tender mercies toward them.

51. Ether Tells Coriantumr to Repent (Ether 6–15)

MAIN CHARACTERS

Ether—The last Jaredite prophet. He told the people to repent to avoid being destroyed. He wrote the final Jaredite records (1:1-6) and hid them (15:33).

Coriantumr—The last Jaredite king and last survivor of his people.

Shiz—The Jaredite army commander during the last battle of that people. He pursued Coriantumr and his army, killing both women and children, and burning cities (14:16–17). He fanatically pursued Coriantumr to avenge his brother's death and to prove that Coriantumr could be killed (14:24).

Moroni—The book of Ether is Moroni's abbreviated account of about 2,000 years of Jaredite history, intermingled with Moroni's personal commentary (for example, his discussion of faith, hope, and charity in Ether 12). He expressed his concern about his feelings of inadequacy (12:23). King Mosiah obtained the plates and then translated them into the Nephite language (Mosiah 28:11–13). They accompanied the brass plates and Nephi's plates until Moroni received them and made an abridgment (Mosiah 28:20; 1:12). Moroni said that he had written only a very little bit of what Ether wrote (15:33).

EVENT 1: The Jaredites Want a King (Ether 6:19–27; 7:1–11)

As Jared and his brother grew old, they gathered their families and asked them what they wanted them to do for them before they died. The descendants wanted them to choose one of their sons to be a king over them.

Jared's brother warned that having a king would lead to captivity (6:23). All of Jared's and his brother's sons refused to be king. Finally, when the people insisted on having a king, one of Jared's sons agreed to become king.

He ruled righteously during his long life (7:1). A succession of kings reigned in cycles of righteousness and wickedness (see Event 2 below). Later, battles between fathers and sons, greed, conspiracies (secret combinations), assassinations, prisons full of people, and rejection of prophets occurred (7–11).

EVENT 2: Cycles of Prosperity and Wickedness (Ether 9)

Throughout the Book of Mormon, cycles of prosperity and wickedness occur (see Story 39's diagram):

1. The people prospered during times of righteousness (9:15–25).
2. The people joined together in secret combinations and turned to wickedness (9:26–27).
3. The Lord sent prophets warning the people of their wickedness (9:28).
4. The people rejected the prophets (9:29).
5. God's judgments fell upon the people (9:30–33).
6. The people humbled themselves and repented, and the Lord blessed them again (9:34–35).

Special note: People can be wealthy and remain righteous, as the Jaredites did for over 225 years (9:15–25). Those reading the Book of Mormon sometimes think it is an account of continuous wars and overlook the generations of peace and righteousness.

EVENT 3: The Prophet Ether (Ether 12:1–5)

Because Ether had the Spirit of the Lord in him, he continually prophesied to the people while Coriantumr was king. He told the people that if they did not believe in God and repent, they would be destroyed. Faith would make them firm in always doing good things, enabling them to be led by God, and to give God glory. Ether prophesied great and marvelous things, which the people did not believe because they could not see them.

EVENT 4: Moroni Defines Faith (Ether 12:6–21)

While translating the Jaredite history, Moroni said that faith is hoping for things you have not seen. You will not know they are true until after your faith has been tested (12:6; also Hebrews 11:1; Alma 32:21). Moroni gives examples of events related to having faith (12:7–22).

EVENT 5: We Are Given Weaknesses That We May Be Humble (Ether 12:23–34)

Moroni was concerned that the Gentiles would mock his poor writing (12:23–26). The Lord told Moroni that fools would mock his writing, but they would be sorry. Humble people would not make fun of others' weaknesses.

The Lord said: (12:27)

If people come unto Jesus Christ . . .	Then, He will show them their weakness. They are given weaknesses so they can be humble.
If people humble themselves and have faith in Him . . .	Then, He will make their weakness become a strength.

Moroni wrote about the importance of faith, hope, and charity (12:28–34).

EVENT 6: Two Jerusalems (Ether 13:1–12)

Ether prophesied of the New Jerusalem and the Old Jerusalem:

- After the Old Jerusalem (where Lehi came from) was destroyed, it would be built again and become a holy city of the Lord for the House of Israel (13:5).

- The New Jerusalem would be built in the Western Hemisphere for the rest of Joseph's descendants (13:6).

- After Christ's Second Coming, the City of Enoch would come down out of heaven and become part of the New Jerusalem (13:3, 10). Those worthy to live in these holy cities will be blessed because their sins will be taken away by Christ's blood (13:10–11).

EVENT 7: War Rages. The Jaredite Civilization is Destroyed (Ether 13:13–15:34)

Ether prophesied to the people, urging them to have faith and repent. The people rejected him and cast him out. He made the remainder of his record while hiding in a small cave during the day and at night saw the destruction happening to his people (13:13–14). The people soon became engaged in wars and secret combinations (13:15–19).

Ether told the king that if he and all of his household did not repent, all the Jaredites would be killed, with the exception of Coriantumr, who would live long enough to see the prophecies come true (13:20–21). Coriantumr refused to repent, and the war continued. To avoid being killed, Ether ran and hid inside the small cave again (13:22).

The battles happened so fast that the dead were not buried, and the smell was so bad it bothered the people day and night (14:22–23). Although Coriantumr lost many battles and was wounded several times, he did not die. Coriantumr, now feeling sad, sent a letter to Shiz, saying that he was willing to give up his kingdom if Shiz would spare his people. Shiz refused. If

Coriantumr gave himself up, Shiz would kill him, and then he would spare the people. Coriantumr and Shiz gathered all the people, including women and children on one side or the other, for a final battle. After days of fighting, only Coriantumr and Shiz remained alive. Shiz fainted from the loss of blood. After Coriantumr rested a little by leaning on his sword, he cut off Shiz's head (15:29–30). Coriantumr collapsed and was unresponsive. He was later discovered by the Nephites and lived another nine months (Omni 1:21).

The Lord told Ether to "go forth." Ether saw that what the Lord had said had come true. He finished writing the Jaredite history and hid the plates (15:33). These plates were found later by the Nephites (Mosiah 8:9–11; Ether 1:1–2). King Mosiah obtained the plates from Limhi's people and then translated them into the Nephite language (Mosiah 28:11–13). They were passed down through the prophets with the brass plates and Nephi's plates until Moroni received them and made an abridgment (Mosiah 28:20; Ether 1:1–2).

OUTCOME: Wickedness Led to Total Destruction

The people's wickedness resulted in a widespread slaughter of people. The final battle resulted in the total destruction of the Jaredites.

52. Moroni Adds to the Records Before Hiding Them (Moroni 1–10)

MAIN CHARACTER

Moroni—A righteous Nephite military commander and the son of Mormon. He was the last Nephite record keeper, having received the plates from his father (Words of Mormon 1:1; Mormon 8:1). He translated and abridged the Jaredite record (Ether 1:1–2) and added his own writings (Mormon 8–9; Moroni 1–6, 10; Title Page) to complete the Book of Mormon. He hid the plates in the hill known as Cumorah. Centuries later, as a resurrected messenger sent from God, he delivered them to Joseph Smith. Not to be confused with Captain Moroni in Stories 28 and 29.

EVENT 1: Practices of the Ancient Church (Moroni 1–6)

- Moroni abridged the Jaredite record contained in the Book of Ether, then decided to record a few more things (1:4).

- Moroni indicated that Christ had given His disciples power to grant the Holy Ghost and had told them how it should be done (2).

- Instructions are given for ordaining priesthood officers (3:1–4).

- Instructions and prayers for administering the sacrament and wine are also given (4:1–5:2 [see Event 2 below]).

- Church administration (6)

    —Repentance, baptism, and taking the name of Christ are the ways to be numbered among the people of God (6:1–4).

    —The purpose and manner of conducting Church meetings under the inspiration of the Holy Ghost are explained (6:5–9).

EVENT 2: The Sacrament Prayers (Moroni 4–5)

Special note: Joseph Smith was instructed that it does not matter what is used in partaking of the sacrament, as long as it is done with the proper intent (see Doctrine and Covenants 27:2–3). Water has now replaced wine because water is plentiful, available, inexpensive, and easy to prepare.

The following two sacrament prayers are quoted directly from the Book of Mormon.

The Blessing on the Bread
(*Special note:* The word *has* replaces *hath* in the Doctrine and Covenants 20:77)
O God, the Eternal Father, we ask thee in the name of thy Son, Jesus Christ, to bless and sanctify this bread to the souls of all those who partake of it; that they may eat in remembrance of the body of thy Son, and witness unto thee, O God, the Eternal Father, that they are willing to take upon them the name of thy Son, and always remember him, and keep his commandments which he hath given them, that they may always have his Spirit to be with them. Amen.

The Blessing on the Wine
(*Special note:* Substitute the term water for wine.)
O God, the Eternal Father, we ask thee in the name of Jesus Christ, to bless and sanctify this wine to the souls of all those who drink of it; that they may do it in remembrance of the blood of thy Son, which was shed for them; that they may witness unto thee, O God, the Eternal Father, that they do always remember him, that they may have his Spirit to be with them. Amen.

EVENT 3: Knowing Good from Evil (Moroni 7:1–19)

Moroni recorded some of his father's words regarding faith, hope, and charity.

- God said you would know what kind of people they were by what they did. If they do good things, then they are good people. Evil people cannot do good things (7:5–6).

- All good comes from God; all bad comes from the devil. The devil is an enemy to God.

Everything that invites a person to do good, to love God and serve Him comes from God (7:12–13).

- The Spirit of Christ (also called the light of Christ) is given to all people so they can know good from evil (7:16). Now that you know the way to judge, by using the light of Christ, be sure you do not judge wrongfully. You will be judged according to how you have judged others (7:18).

EVENT 4: Faith, Hope, and Charity (Moroni 7:40–48)

What should you hope for? You should hope to be raised to eternal life through Christ's Atonement and the power of His resurrection. So if you have faith, you also have hope. Without faith there is no hope. You cannot have faith and hope unless you are humble. If you are proud, your faith and hope will do you no good before God. If you are humble, and confess by the Holy Ghost's power that Jesus is the Christ, this means you have charity. If you do not have charity, you are nothing, because charity never fails. Hold on to charity, the greatest gift of all, because everything else will fail. Charity is the pure love of Christ, and it will last forever.

How can we acquire charity? By praying to the Father with all the energy of your heart, that you will be filled with this love (7:48).

EVENT 5: Infant Baptism (Moroni 8:11–23)

Little children do not need to repent; they do not need to be baptized (8:11). Whoever says that little children need baptism is saying that Christ does not have mercy, and that His sacrifice (the Atonement) does not mean anything (8:20). People who do not know God's commandments cannot repent, and they will not be judged by what they do not know. Baptism is not for them, it is for people who know God's commandments and can repent (8:22).

EVENT 6: The Holy Ghost Testifies of All Truth (Moroni 10)

Moroni's advice:

- Remember how much mercy God has had on people since the time of Adam and Eve (10:3).

- When you read this book (known today as the Book of Mormon), ask God the Father in Christ's name if it is true (10:4). You can know the truth of all things by the power of the Holy Ghost (10:5).

- Do not deny God's power (10:7).

- Remember that every good gift comes from Christ (10:18).

- Remember that Christ is the same yesterday, today and forever (10:19).

- Remember Moroni's words (10:27).

- Come to Christ (10:30).

EVENT 7: Gifts Follow Those Who Come Unto Christ (Moroni 10:8–19)

- Do not deny God's gifts. There are many gifts, and they work in different ways. They are given to people for their good and as a blessing to others who benefit from them (10:8).

- All gifts come by the Spirit of Christ, and they are given to people as Christ thinks best. Remember, every good gift comes from Christ (10:17–18).

- Come to Christ. Do not let yourselves do wicked things. If you keep God's commandments, and love Him with all your heart, mind, and strength, His grace will make you perfect in Him. (10:30, 32).

OUTCOME:

Summary of the instructions on how to:

• Judge between good and evil.

• Receive a testimony of the gospel and the Book of Mormon.

• Understand and acquire the spiritual gifts available to us.

• Come unto Christ and be perfected in Him.

• Have faith, hope, and charity.

Moroni said farewell to all. He said he would soon rest in God's paradise until his spirit and body reunite again (be resurrected). He will meet us at the judgment bar in front of Jehovah, the Eternal Judge (10:34).

APPENDIX A: The Law of Justice and the Law of Mercy Are Essential to Understanding the Atonement

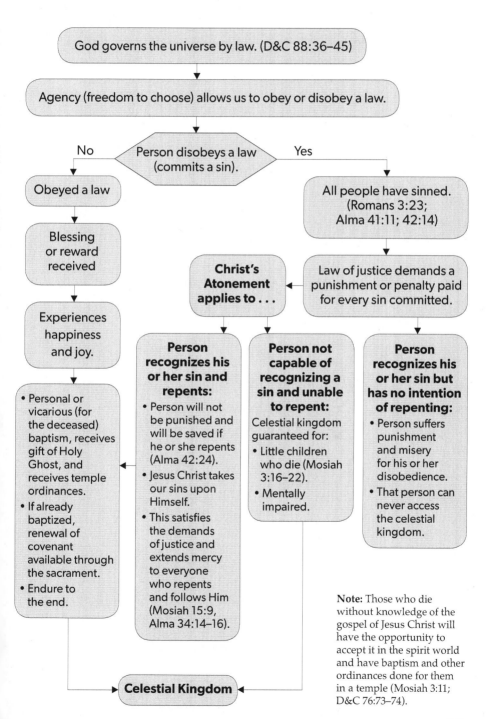

God governs the universe by law. (D&C 88:36–45)

Agency (freedom to choose) allows us to obey or disobey a law.

Person disobeys a law (commits a sin).

No → Obeyed a law

Yes → All people have sinned. (Romans 3:23; Alma 41:11; 42:14)

Obeyed a law
→ Blessing or reward received
→ Experiences happiness and joy.
→ • Personal or vicarious (for the deceased) baptism, receives gift of Holy Ghost, and receives temple ordinances.
• If already baptized, renewal of covenant available through the sacrament.
• Endure to the end.

Law of justice demands a punishment or penalty paid for every sin committed.

Christ's Atonement applies to . . .

Person recognizes his or her sin and repents:
• Person will not be punished and will be saved if he or she repents (Alma 42:24).
• Jesus Christ takes our sins upon Himself.
• This satisfies the demands of justice and extends mercy to everyone who repents and follows Him (Mosiah 15:9, Alma 34:14–16).

Person not capable of recognizing a sin and unable to repent:
Celestial kingdom guaranteed for:
• Little children who die (Mosiah 3:16–22).
• Mentally impaired.

Person recognizes his or her sin but has no intention of repenting:
• Person suffers punishment and misery for his or her disobedience.
• That person can never access the celestial kingdom.

Note: Those who die without knowledge of the gospel of Jesus Christ will have the opportunity to accept it in the spirit world and have baptism and other ordinances done for them in a temple (Mosiah 3:11; D&C 76:73–74).

Celestial Kingdom

APPENDIX B: Repentance

Key: Bold numbers in parentheses are the major steps for repentance.

- God governs the universe by law (D&C 88:36–45).
- Spirit (Light) of Christ is given to all to know good from evil (Moroni 7:16, 18–19).
- People are taught enough to know good from evil (2 Nephi 2:5).
- Agency (freedom to choose) allows us to obey or disobey a law.
- All people have sinned (Romans 3:23; Alma 41:11; 42:14).

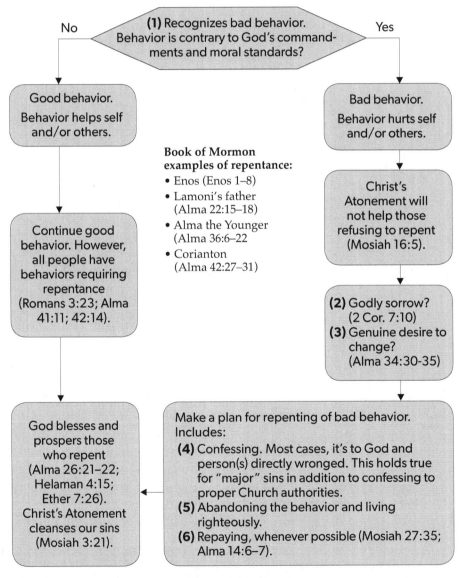

(1) Recognizes bad behavior. Behavior is contrary to God's commandments and moral standards?

No → Good behavior. Behavior helps self and/or others.

Yes → Bad behavior. Behavior hurts self and/or others.

Continue good behavior. However, all people have behaviors requiring repentance (Romans 3:23; Alma 41:11; 42:14).

Book of Mormon examples of repentance:
- Enos (Enos 1–8)
- Lamoni's father (Alma 22:15–18)
- Alma the Younger (Alma 36:6–22
- Corianton (Alma 42:27–31)

Christ's Atonement will not help those refusing to repent (Mosiah 16:5).

(2) Godly sorrow? (2 Cor. 7:10)
(3) Genuine desire to change? (Alma 34:30-35)

God blesses and prospers those who repent (Alma 26:21–22; Helaman 4:15; Ether 7:26). Christ's Atonement cleanses our sins (Mosiah 3:21).

Make a plan for repenting of bad behavior. Includes:
(4) Confessing. Most cases, it's to God and person(s) directly wronged. This holds true for "major" sins in addition to confessing to proper Church authorities.
(5) Abandoning the behavior and living righteously.
(6) Repaying, whenever possible (Mosiah 27:35; Alma 14:6–7).

APPENDIX C: Three Kinds of Hell
First Spiritual Death, Spirit Prison, Second Spiritual Death

This table was adapted from an unknown source.

	First Spiritual Death
Where?	Mortality; earth-life
How long?	It is a temporary spiritual death. From age of accountability to physical death
Who?	The first spiritual death is the actual separation from the immediate presence of God, first experienced by Adam and Eve and consequently by their descendants (Helaman 1:16). Anyone who knowingly violates God's laws suffers some degree of hell equal to the seriousness of the sin. Those not repenting may experience the pain of hell in this life as well as the next (1 Nephi 16:2; Alma 40:14).
How to be rescued?	This will happen through faith in Christ, repentance, and obedience to the laws and ordinances of Christ's gospel because of His Atonement (2 Nephi 1:13; 9:45; Enos 1:6; Mosiah 4:3). All mortals will be saved from this death through Christ's Atonement and resurrection (2 Nephi 9:10–15; Helaman 14:15-19), to be brought back into God's presence. Christ suffered so He could deliver everyone from hell (Alma 7:11–13; 33:23).
What is experienced?	Mental misery will be associated with a regretful realization of one's disobedience to God's laws (Mosiah 2:38; Alma 36:12–16). Suffering is described as "guilt, and pain, and anguish, which is like an unquenchable fire" (Mosiah 2:38).

Spirit Prison	
Where?	Postmortal world for those who were disobedient in this mortal life. One of two divisions of the spirit world between death and the resurrection: paradise for the righteous, "hell" for the unrighteous (Alma 40:12–13).
How long?	Temporary spiritual death. Between physical death and the resurrection (2 Nephi 9:10-12). Individuals will be released after they have paid the penalty for their sins.
Who?	People who were disobedient during their life on earth and failed to keep God's commandments (Alma 12:12–16, 32; Helaman 14:18). The gospel will be taught, and those in this state will have an opportunity to repent and accept the ordinances of salvation that are performed for them in a temple (D&C 138:30–35). The devil and his followers as well as the spirits of mortals who died unrepentant will reside here.
How to be rescued?	Individual spirits will be cleansed, will cease to experience mental torment, and will be resurrected with their physical bodies. Many of these spirits will enter into the telestial kingdom in their resurrected state (2 Nephi 9:10–12).
What is experienced?	They will suffer misery (mental torment) while awaiting the resurrection: "weeping, and wailing, and gnashing of teeth" (Mosiah 3:25–27; 2 Nephi 2:27–29; 9:16; Alma 12:16–18).

Second Spiritual Death	
Where?	A place for those who cannot be cleansed by Jesus Christ's atonement because they committed the unforgivable and unpardonable sin (1 Nephi 15:35).
How long?	Permanent spiritual death. Only this kind of hell continues to operate after the resurrection and final judgment
Who?	The devil and his followers, including the sons of perdition (those who committed the unforgiveable and unpardonable sin) (1 Nephi 15:35). The fate of those who have not repented is determined on the final judgment day (Alma 12:16–36).
How to be rescued?	Will not be rescued. Occupants will continue in spiritual darkness. Occupants do not inherit some degree of glory.
What is experienced?	They will suffer hell continuously, even after the resurrection. The devil will "reign" over those who have suffered a permanent spiritual death. They will enter "into a state of misery and endless torment," which "torment is as a lake of fire and brimstone" (Mosiah 3:25–27; 2 Nephi 2:27–29; 9:16; Alma 12:16–18).

Appendix D: 25 Examples of the Book of Mormon's Teachings

These 25 scripture passages provide a few of the important Book of Mormon teachings. They quote directly from the Book of Mormon.

1. The Lord prepares a way to obey His commandments.

1 Nephi 3:7—"And it came to pass that I, Nephi, said unto my father: I will go and do the things which the Lord hath commanded, for I know that the Lord giveth no commandments unto the children of men, save he shall prepare a way for them that they may accomplish the thing which he commandeth them."

2. Adam fell that men might be.

2 Nephi 2:22–25—"And now, behold, if Adam had not transgressed he would not have fallen, but he would have remained in the garden of Eden. And all things which were created must have remained in the same state in which they were after they were created; and they must have remained forever, and had no end.

"And they would have had no children; wherefore they would have remained in a state of innocence, having no joy, for they knew no misery; doing no good, for they knew no sin.

"But behold, all things have been done in the wisdom of him who knoweth all things.

"Adam fell that men might be; and men are, that they might have joy."

3. We are free to choose.

2 Nephi 2:27—"Wherefore, men are free according to the flesh; and all things are given them which are expedient unto man. And they are free to choose liberty and eternal life, through the great Mediator of all men, or to choose captivity and death, according to the captivity and power of the devil; for he seeketh that all men might be miserable like unto himself."

4. All are alike unto God.

2 Nephi 26:33—"For none of these iniquities come of the Lord; for he doeth that which is good among the children of men; and he doeth nothing save it be plain unto the children of men; and he inviteth them all to come unto him and partake of his goodness; and he denieth none that come unto him, black and white, bond and free, male and female; and he remembereth the heathen; and all are alike unto God, both Jew and Gentile."

5. God gives knowledge line upon line.

2 Nephi 28:30—"For behold, thus saith the Lord God: I will give unto the children of men line upon line, precept upon precept, here a little and there a little; and blessed are those who hearken unto my precepts, and lend an ear unto my counsel, for they shall learn wisdom; for unto him that receiveth I will give more; and from them that shall say, We have enough, from them shall be taken away even that which they have."

6. If we feast upon the words of Christ, we can know all things that we should do.

2 Nephi 32:3—"Angels speak by the power of the Holy Ghost; wherefore, they speak the words of Christ. Wherefore, I said unto you, feast upon the words of Christ; for behold, the words of Christ will tell you all things what ye should do."

7. If we pray always, God will consecrate our performance for the welfare of our souls.

2 Nephi 32:8–9—"And now, my beloved brethren, I perceive that ye ponder still in your hearts; and it grieveth me that I must speak concerning this thing. For if ye would hearken unto the Spirit which teacheth a man to pray, ye would know that ye must pray; for the evil spirit teacheth not a man to pray, but teacheth him that he must not pray.

"But behold, I say unto you that ye must pray always, and not faint; that ye must not perform any thing unto the Lord save in the first place ye shall pray unto the Father in the name of Christ, that he will consecrate thy performance unto thee, that thy performance may be for the welfare of thy soul."

8. By serving others we serve God.

Mosiah 2:17—"And behold, I tell you these things that ye may learn wisdom; that ye may learn that when ye are in the service of your fellow beings ye are only in the service of your God."

9. Obedience brings blessings and happiness.

Mosiah 2:41—"And moreover, I would desire that ye should consider on the blessed and happy state of those that keep the commandments of God. For behold, they are blessed in all things, both temporal and spiritual; and if they hold out faithful to the end they are received into heaven, that thereby they may dwell with God in a state of never-ending happiness. O remember, remember that these things are true; for the Lord God hath spoken it."

10. Put off the natural man and become a Saint through the Atonement.

Mosiah 3:19—"For the natural man is an enemy to God, and has been from the fall of Adam, and will be, forever and ever, unless he yields to the enticings of the Holy Spirit, and putteth off the natural man and becometh a saint through the atonement of Christ the Lord, and becometh as a child, submissive, meek, humble, patient, full of love, willing to submit to all things which the Lord seeth fit to inflict upon him, even as a child doth submit to his father."

11. Believe in God and that He has all wisdom.

Mosiah 4:9—"Believe in God; believe that he is, and that he created all things, both in heaven and in earth; believe that he has all wisdom, and all power, both in heaven and in earth; believe that man doth not comprehend all the things which the Lord can comprehend."

12. Through baptism we enter a covenant with God.

Mosiah 18:8–10—"And it came to pass that he said unto them: Behold, here are the waters of Mormon (for thus were they called) and now, as ye are desirous to come into the fold of God, and to be called his people, and are willing to bear one another's burdens, that they may be light;

"Yea, and are willing to mourn with those that mourn; yea, and comfort those that stand in need of comfort, and to stand as witnesses of God at all times and in all things, and in all places that ye may be in, even until death, that ye may be redeemed of God, and be numbered with those of the first resurrection, that ye may have eternal life—

"Now I say unto you, if this be the desire of your hearts, what have you against being baptized in the name of the Lord, as a witness before him that ye have entered into a covenant with him, that ye will serve him and keep his commandments, that he may pour out his Spirit more abundantly upon you?"

13. Jesus Christ experienced our pains and overcame sin and death.

Alma 7:11–13—"And he shall go forth, suffering pains and afflictions and temptations of every kind; and this that the word might be fulfilled which saith he will take upon him the pains and the sicknesses of his people.

"And he will take upon him death, that he may loose the bands of death which bind his people; and he will take upon him their infirmities, that his bowels may be filled with mercy, according to the flesh, that he may know according to the flesh how to succor his people according to their infirmities.

"Now the Spirit knoweth all things; nevertheless the Son of God suffereth according to the flesh that he might take upon him the sins of his people, that he might blot out their transgressions according to the power of his deliverance; and now behold, this is the testimony which is in me."

14. There must be an Atonement made.

Alma 34:9–10—"For it is expedient that an atonement should be made; for according to the great plan of the Eternal God there must be an atonement made, or else all mankind must unavoidably perish; yea, all are hardened; yea, all are fallen and are lost, and must perish except it be through the atonement which it is expedient should be made.

"For it is expedient that there should be a great and last sacrifice; yea, not a sacrifice of man, neither of beast, neither of any manner of fowl; for it shall not be a human sacrifice; but it must be an infinite and eternal sacrifice."

15. Go no more after the lust of your eyes.

Alma 39:9—"Now my son, I would that ye should repent and forsake your sins, and go no more after the lusts of your eyes, but cross yourself in all these things; for except ye do this ye can in nowise inherit the kingdom of God. Oh, remember, and take it upon you, and cross yourself in these things."

16. Wickedness never was happiness.

Alma 41:10—"Do not suppose, because it has been spoken concerning restoration, that ye shall be restored from sin to happiness. Behold, I say unto you, wickedness never was happiness."

17. Build your foundation on Christ.

Helaman 5:12—"And now, my sons, remember, remember that it is upon the rock of our Redeemer, who is Christ, the Son of God, that ye must build your foundation; that when the devil shall send forth his mighty winds, yea, his shafts in the whirlwind, yea, when all his hail and his mighty storm shall beat upon you, it shall have no power over you to drag you down to the gulf of misery and endless wo, because of the rock upon which ye are built, which is a sure foundation, a foundation whereon if men build they cannot fall."

18. Jesus Christ suffered the will of the Father in all things.

3 Nephi 11:10–11—"Behold, I am Jesus Christ, whom the prophets testified shall come into the world.

"And behold, I am the light and the life of the world; and I have drunk out of that bitter cup which the Father hath given me, and have glorified the Father in taking upon me the sins of the world, in the which I have suffered the will of the Father in all things from the beginning."

19. Jesus Christ invites us to become perfect.

3 Nephi 12:48—"Therefore I would that ye should be perfect even as I, or your Father who is in heaven is perfect."

20. Watch and pray always in the name of Jesus Christ.

3 Nephi 18:15, 20–21—"Verily, verily, I say unto you, ye must watch and pray always, lest ye be tempted by the devil, and ye be led away captive by him.

"And whatsoever ye shall ask the Father in my name, which is right, believing that ye shall receive, behold it shall be given unto you.

"Pray in your families unto the Father, always in my name, that your wives and your children may be blessed."

21. Be baptized and sanctified by receiving the Holy Ghost.

3 Nephi 27:20—"Now this is the commandment: Repent, all ye ends of the earth, and come unto me and be baptized in my name, that ye may be sanctified by the reception of the Holy Ghost, that ye may stand spotless before me at the last day."

22. A witness comes after the trial of faith.

Ether 12:6—"And now, I, Moroni, would speak somewhat concerning these things; I would show unto the world that faith is things which are hoped for and not seen; wherefore, dispute not because ye see not, for ye receive no witness until after the trial of your faith."

23. The Savior can make weak things strong.

Ether 12:27—"And if men come unto me I will show unto them their weakness. I give unto men weakness that they may be humble; and my grace is sufficient for all men that humble themselves before me; for if they humble themselves before me, and have faith in me, then will I make weak things become strong unto them."

24. Charity is the pure love of Christ.

Moroni 7:45, 47–48—"And charity suffereth long, and is kind, and envieth not, and is not puffed up, seeketh not her own, is not easily provoked, thinketh no evil, and rejoiceth not in iniquity but rejoiceth in the truth, beareth all things, believeth all things, hopeth all things, endureth all things.

"But charity is the pure love of Christ, and it endureth forever; and whoso is found possessed of it at the last day, it shall be well with him.

"Wherefore, my beloved brethren, pray unto the Father with all the energy of heart, that ye may be filled with this love, which he hath bestowed upon all who are true followers of his Son, Jesus Christ; that ye may become the sons of God; that when he shall appear we shall be like him, for we shall see him as he is; that we may have this hope; that we may be purified even as he is pure."

25. The Holy Ghost reveals truth to those who ask God with real intent.

Moroni 10:4–5—"And when ye shall receive these things, I would exhort you that ye would ask God, the Eternal Father, in the name of Christ, if these things are not true; and if ye shall ask with a sincere heart, with real intent, having faith in Christ, he will manifest the truth of it unto you, by the power of the Holy Ghost.

"And by the power of the Holy Ghost ye may know the truth of all things."

Works Cited

Black, Susan Easton. *400 Questions and Answers About the Book of Mormon* (American Fork, Utah: Covenant Communications, 2011).

Gaskill, Alonzo L. *Miracles of the Book of Mormon* (Springville, Utah: CFI, 2015).

Hamblin, William J. "History of Warfare in the Book of Mormon" in Daniel H. Ludlow, ed. *Encyclopedia of Mormonism* (New York: Macmillan Publishing Company, 1992).

Hardy, Grant R. "Book of Mormon Plates and Records," in Daniel H. Ludlow, ed. *Encyclopedia of Mormonism* (New York: Macmillan Publishing Company, 1992).

Ludlow, Daniel H. *A Companion to Your Study of the Book of Mormon* (Salt Lake City, Utah: Deseret Book, 1976).

Millet, Robert L. "Plain and Precious Things." in Dennis L. Largey, ed. *Book of Mormon Reference Companion* (Salt Lake City, Utah: Deseret Book, 2003).

Nyman, Monte S. "Book of Mormon," in Daniel H. Ludlow, ed. *Encyclopedia of Mormonism* (New York: Macmillan Publishing Company, 1992).

Ogden, D. Kelly and Andrew C. Skinner. *Verse by Verse: The Book of Mormon, Volume 2* (Salt Lake City, Utah: Deseret Book, 2011).

Smith, Joseph. *History of The Church of Jesus Christ of Latter-day Saints.* Edited by B. H. Roberts. Ed. Rev. (Salt Lake City, Utah: The Church of Jesus Christ of Latter-day Saints, 1932–51).

Thorne Melvin J. "Complexity, Consistency, Ignorance, and Probabilities," in Noel B. Reynolds, ed., *Book of Mormon Authorship Revisited: The Evidence for Ancient Origins,* (Provo: FARMS, 1997).

Welch, John W. "Timing the Translation of the Book of Mormon: 'Days [and Hours] Never to Be Forgotten.'" *BYU Studies Quarterly* 57, no. 4 (2018).